5 16 45

arch.

D0460600

A Theory for Practice

A Theory for Practice

Architecture in Three Discourses

Bill Hubbard Jr.

The MIT Press
Cambridge, Massachusetts
London, England

This book was set in New Baskerville by Graphic Composition, Inc. and was printed and bound in the United States of America.

Library of Congress Cataloging-in-Publication data

Hubbard, Bill, 1947–
    A Theory for practice : architecture in three discourses / Bill Hubbard, Jr.
       p. cm.
    Includes bibliographical references and index.
    ISBN 0-262-08235-7
    1. Architectural design—Philosophy.   I. Title.
  NA2750.H84   1995
  720′.1—dc20   94-23717
                                                          CIP

Quotations from *On the Art of Building in Ten Books* by Leon Battista Alberti (Joseph Rykwert, trans.) © 1988 by The MIT Press. Used by permission.

Quotations from *After Virtue: A Study in Moral Theory*, rev. ed., by Alasdair MacIntyre ©1984 by University of Notre Dame Press. Used by permission.

Quotations from *Old Jules* ©1935, 1963 by Mari Sandoz. Reprinted by permission of McIntosh and Otis, Inc.

Quotations from *A Thousand Acres* by Jane Smiley ©1991 by Jane Smiley. Reprinted by permission of Alfred A. Knopf, Inc.

For Gary, *sine qua non*.

Contents

Acknowledgments   ix

Introduction: Thinking Like an Architect   1

1 Other Ways to Think about a Building   17

1a Thinking about Results   17

1b Thinking about Values   28

2 Getting Specific about Other Ways of Thinking   39

2a From Results to the Market   39

2b From Values to Community   61

3 A Way to Think about Practice   87

4 Working with Other Ways of Thinking   101

5 Talking across Ways of Thinking   121

6 The Good Life for an Architect   149

Notes   169

Index   177

Acknowledgments

People who don't write often ask people who do (it's their kind way of showing interest), "When did you begin your book?" Unlike most writers, I can answer with precision: "At 10 A.M. on June 24, 1987, over cappuccino in a plaza on Via Carini in Trastevere." And although the ideas of that morning occupy only a tiny part of one chapter, they grew, as ideas can, to become my whole book. So it's with real gratitude that I acknowledge the grant from the Jeptha and Emily Wade Fund that made that moment in Rome, and the summer in Europe that followed it, possible. I am doubly indebted because the tag end of that same grant made possible the 1992 trip to Nebraska that furnished the emotional heart of the book.

I'm also indebted to my readers—Bill Morrish and Catherine Brown (whose guest-room nightstand furnished two absolutely crucial books), Bob Campbell, and Tom Chastain—and to the anonymous readers of The MIT Press review process, whose comments disciplined the final shape of the book.

And I would be sorely remiss if I did not acknowledge the support—moral and otherwise—of the wait staff and bar staff of Bertucci's and the late-lamented Marcella's in Boston. Without their comfort to look forward to, the solitary days of writing and rewriting could not have been borne.

Introduction: Thinking Like an Architect

The scene is the 1992 convention of the American Institute of Architects, held in Boston's big convention center just blocks from my apartment. The main events at these gatherings are of course the seminars, the dinners, and the vast trade show. But the AIA charges corporate-tax-deduction rates for admission to those things, and so I content myself with roaming the corridors and exhibits. Ambling with me are hundreds of other architects, each freighted with handouts and product literature, most of them unwittingly overdressed for an unseasonably warm Boston June. The overdress, though, is of that kind displayed only by us architects, and perhaps legible in its meaning only to us.

To the uninitiated, this might seem to be merely a crowd of uncommonly well-dressed people. Seeing the number of men wearing tattersall shirts with knit ties and suede shoes, they might wonder how a look of the early 1960s could hold sway for so long. But they would also note other men in suits of an exquisite Italian slouch or assured British drape. And they would see women in the flowing dresses and artisanal jewelry usually reserved for major art openings.

But to us architects these clothes would signify more. We would know that these striking ensembles had not been merely well chosen and coordinated. They had been *designed*, each a kind of self-appointed architectural commission, which had proceeded from a "site analysis" of the possibilities inherent in physical qualities, to a "design synthesis" that would orchestrate those qualities in the service of an imagined self-conception.

That man over there didn't just happen upon his Armani suit. He has consciously observed the way he slouches, and in fact takes a secret delight in that particular posture (and has done so in all the days since his mother told him to "Sit up straight!"). He knows that this carefully unconstructed bag of cloth will amplify his slouch, make it seem paradoxically both relaxed and compelling.

That woman knows she has large, strong features. As a girl she had yearned for Sandra Dee perkiness, but she got over that in college. She knows now that oversized jewelry and bold makeup will make those big features seem part of an orchestrated ensemble, and that the effect can be made to seem "monumental" with a dress of tent-like silhouette.

That man across the way noticed, at about age thirty, that he was developing a premature white shock in his hair, just above his left eyebrow. Recognizing its potential value, he had grown his hair longer and adopted dark shirts and unpatterned ties. Today, years later, he has his graying hair carefully tinted around that white shock.

I engage in this bit of pop-psych reportage not out of a desire to set myself above such ploys (I have my own strategies for dealing with a fullish face), nor to hold this crowd up to ridicule. If that were my intention, it would be all too easy to lampoon what patently is a scene of self-display. No, I tell this story out of a deep and unabashed affection for these members of my profession. For while others might see vanity, what I saw on display in that convention hall was an earnest faith in the power of design. Those conventioners believed that not just your clothes and not just your surroundings, but your meals and even your daily schedule are properly objects of design. And if all of your life can be consciously and beautifully wrought, then that will be a better life, for you and for all who might be touched by you.

If that is so, if those clothes were the outer and visible emblem of an inner and hidden system of belief, then what are those beliefs, and how do they come about? To understand what and why architects believe, you have to walk for a while in their (designer) shoes, see some of the experiences that shaped them. If you could understand those experiences, you'd understand why, when those architects were designing their convention wardrobes, the images in their minds (in that season after *Pretty Woman*) had probably not been Richard Gere and Julia Roberts. More likely it had been people like Frank Lloyd Wright and Ray Eames they were thinking about as they packed their suitcases for the flight to Boston.

Wright was certainly known for his clothes—those custom-made suits, the cane and shoes, the porkpie hat. But equally famous, and much more telling, was the life he orchestrated for himself and his followers at the two Taliesins. Not just the buildings and surroundings but every accouterment of life there was carefully designed. The days were designed as well—the directed frenzy of working hours that gave way to evenings of ease and reflection, with their ceremonious dinners, discussions, and musicales presided over by Frank and Olgivanna.

Ray Eames too designed the image she would present to the world. In later years she seemed always to appear in tight-bodiced, full-skirted shirtwaists, of a severe cut and all in the muted colors that come from natural dyes. But as with Wright, the clothes were only the visible emblem of a larger, deeper life. And for a generation of California architects, an afternoon at the famous Case Study house was a lived reaffirmation of the ability of design to render a life exquisite.

It was not just the house and its promise of a better world, nor was it the house's qualities of light and space and restraint. And it was not just the collections of found objects arrayed casually (but with museum-case beauty) on tabletops and shelves. It was not so much the house that made an impression, it was the way life was lived there. It was the vases of roses—the old, heavy-fragranced kind, always in a mixture of colors, each rose perfect and fully blown, just on the point of dropping its petals. And it was the tea, served on the terrace from an old-fashioned china pot into delicate cups. And always sweets, but not just any sweets: with the tea there would be a great panettone, or biscotti, or millefeuilles. Or berries, a very few but each fresh-picked, with thick cream, eaten with big sterling dessert spoons. And all of this while looking out over the tawny grass toward a sliver of the Pacific, the whole moment accompanied by the rustle and smell of eucalyptus trees. As the light faded and it came time to leave, you would float reluctantly away; and for hours—days—thereafter you would catch yourself trying, in small gestures, to recreate that world in your own life.

Charles and Ray Eames in the living room of their Case Study house (courtesy Lucia
Eames Demetrios dba Eames Office ©1994)

I would venture to say that every architect has his or her own version of my Ray Eames story, either in some personal acquaintance, or in a book- or building-engendered imagining, or in the experience of a glancing encounter (a lecture, say) that confirmed and vivified prior expectations about the kind of world that design can open.

If you are not an architect, nevertheless you too have probably had a similar epiphany—perhaps a conversation in later years with a great teacher of your early days. In that encounter you were brought to remember how, when she had spoken in the classroom, the chaos of your young life had come to make sense. She had seemed, then, to possess a system of ideas, and with those ideas she had always been able to give you an explanation of why things happened as they did. Talking with her now, you could see that the whole of her life had emanated from that system of ideas, had been in fact a lived confirmation of them.

On reflection, though, you realize that her life hadn't just flowed unbidden from those ideas; she had at some point resolved to live her life so as to enact them into reality. Her life had *instanced* those ideas. She had taken what were mere abstractions and lived them into a kind of realness that could be experienced by all she touched, most especially you.

"To have such a life!" we say to ourselves, for two very human desires are joined when we can bring ourselves to live by a system of ideas. The world around us makes sense. And our own life, as an instantiation of those sense-making ideas, seems purposive, meaningful, exquisite.

Design is such a system of ideas. And what I and others felt at the Eames house, what Wright's followers felt at Taliesin, was the experience of design ideas being instanced, enacted into convincing, exquisite reality.

It's a human temptation to suppose that because something works for you, it would work equally well for everybody. Architects, being human after all, are tempted to believe that because the designed life gives them such satisfaction, then anyone could have as good a life.

If it's a human temptation to consider your experience universally applicable, professionals are doubly lured in this direction by the efficacy of their expertise. Told of an argument between newlyweds, an attorney in contract law might catch himself thinking, "If only they'd worked out the contingencies beforehand . . ." Other professionals—accountants, clergy, psychiatrists, entrepreneurs—are likewise drawn to the thought that if their knowledge and values could only be applied across the board, the world would be a better place.

The architectural profession, though, has the explicit charge to design "better places," so we are tempted by opportunity as well as belief. Our professional lives persuade us of the applicability of our beliefs, and the world seems, by its actions, to invite us to apply them.

And if all that weren't enough to lead an architect to believe that design values are universally applicable, there is the matter of the architect's education. In other professions, a student might succumb to the belief that his education explains how the world works (our contract-law attorney in his student days), but architects are explicitly told that their education gives them the knowledge and values needed to diagnose the human condition. Virtually every architect now in practice received this message in school, in one of three versions.

The first version, the most venerable, is the modernist project itself. Now a century-and-a-half old by some measures, modernism is a phenomenon so multifaceted and multi-interpreted as to defeat any attempt I might make at a comprehensive or generally acceptable description. But our concern here is not so much to reveal the true nature of architectural modernism as it is to show how modernism serves architects as a tradition of belief. This second task is much the easier, for virtually all the tenets of the tradition are contained in two "sacred texts," Nikolaus Pevsner's *Pioneers of Modern Design* and Siegfried Giedion's *Space, Time and Architecture.*

For virtually every American architect who graduated before 1970, these books described what architecture is, how it got to be that way, and what it is supposed to do in the world. They told the story of how William Morris had begun the struggle for modernism in the mid-nineteenth century, how Louis Sullivan and Frank Lloyd Wright had carried it forward to the time of the Bauhaus and Le Corbusier, and how modernism had achieved its triumph in the years following World War II.

The books argued that traditional patterns of building and living had endured into the present age, where they no longer accorded with our needs. If we could learn to discount the habits of tradition and look only at those human needs, we could, through rational analysis, derive new and more suitable patterns of building and living. If we could then make those patterns visible, instance them, people would apprehend those new patterns and, appreciating their good sense, willingly bring their lives into accord with them. Design would diagnose how we live, prescribe how we should live, and through form, give us the surroundings that would speak that new life—a life that, the scales having fallen from our eyes, we would live with the enthusiasm of the converted.

We in the profession know that this heroic vision of modernism has been thoroughly discredited, by both scholarly studies and subsequent events. Scholars showed up the diagnostic methods as not truly rational, but the more telling argument was that the environments produced by modernism, whether rational or not, felt void of meaning.

But even though discredited, the modernist project wasn't simply thrown out. People are loath to abandon a belief system that has made satisfying sense of their world, even when those beliefs are put into crisis. Often in such a situation people will try to recast the core of their belief so that it can handle the perceived crisis while remaining in place. The core of modernist belief had been that design could diagnose the human condition. If a lack of meaning was the source of the crisis, could diagnosis be recast to produce meaning and so survive as a core of belief?

It could (and this became the second version of architectural education) because *tradition* could be seen as a source of meaning. (Discounting tradition had been modernism's mistake, according to this view, not its belief in diagnosis.) Under this new conception, design would look at traditional habits of building and living and, through a scrutiny almost indistinguishable from diagnosis, reveal the deep patterns that lay beneath those habits and imbued them with meaning. Design would then make those patterns visible to us, instance them, so that we would not just *have* them (as we would with unself-conscious "traditional" building); we would have them in ways that made us aware of their presence around us. In sensing them, we would be brought to a vivid awareness of the ways in which those patterns accorded with how we lived. And in sensing that connection, we would then live consciously—not in accord with mere habit, but in accord with patterns revealed to us by design.

In this reformulated mode, diagnosis-by-design opened to architects ideas of sacred and profane space, dwelling as a universal human need, the patterns behind existing urban contexts—and convinced many that those were the concepts with which we architects should design. For many graduates after 1970, this bundle of ideas became part of a new belief structure, its inherent heterodoxy felt to be not a defect but a fitting reflection of real-life diversity (and, as well, a proper redress for the hubris of modernism's claims to universality through rationalism).

But the reaction to modernism gave rise to yet another conception of design's ability to diagnose the human condition. In advanced bookstores you will now find—usually in the section formerly denoted "Literary Criticism"—an enlarged section labeled "Critical Theory," its linear footage dominated by authors like Lacan, Baudrillard, Foucault, Derrida. In such books are contained the core principles of the movement to *deconstruct* accepted presumptions about how things got to be the way they are. The central insight of critical theory is that meaning itself—the way we explain what happens around us and thus how we act in response—is a constructed thing. It is constructed not by a process of disinterested truth testing but by the actions, sometimes even inadvertent, of Power. Power controls us not merely through the overt exercise of its influence, but through the more invidious (and harder to spot) process of determining how we make sense of the world.

Design theorists adopting these methods made the case that modernist ideas had unwittingly served the ends of Power: it was in Power's interest to have people portrayed as only functionalist "needers of facilities" and thus consumers of the products Power supplied. These theorists made the further case that traditions are not true repositories of meaning because Power lets survive only those traditions that don't threaten its ends. But, these theorists said, with the tools of deconstruction it is possible to get *behind* the levers of Power.

From that position design can unmask Power, show where it has distorted our perceptions, and thus get at true, uninfluenced meaning.

And so we have the third version (offered now in advanced schools) of how design can diagnose life. Design can uncover patterns uninfluenced by Power. If those patterns were to be built in the world (or shown to us in drawing or model form), people would see the stark contrast between them and the world given to us by Power. Sensing the rightness of those new patterns and the truth they reveal, people would naturally choose to reform their lives to be free of the untruth that, before it had been deconstructed, had been invisible to them.

We now might begin to understand what was in the minds of those architects at the AIA convention.

• All of them had found, early in life, that they were moved by the experience of designed things.

• Many had had design epiphanies that showed them a vision of the serene harmony that can result when both life and surroundings are animated by ideas of design.

• All had had an education where they encountered a community of people who shared, and thus validated, their feelings for designed things and the designed life.

• In those schools they had found that delight in designed things was something they themselves could engender, with objects of their own creation.

• There they had been shown that not just delight but humanistic purpose, consciously felt, is the condition that can result when design can put forth its interpretations of the world.

• And finally, all had gone into offices (and now to this convention) where they had found all their views supported anew, by a community of people who shared their enthusiasms, their values, their jokes, their heroes, and (except for a few quibbles) their vision of what design can do in the world.

Who, in the face of all this, could resist believing that she had hold of something deeply important, deeply right for all people?

Who could resist?

The answer, well known to architects whether at the convention or not, is that their design ideas almost daily meet resistance—and misunderstanding, dismissal, even outright disdain. And this, from the very people who, they had been told and believed, would be *helped* by those ideas.

Of course it's not hard to imagine the kinds of thinking that would resist design ideas. All that's required is that we step out of our designer shoes and look at the situation from a perspective outside the corridors of the convention. It's a perspective, by the way, that my fellow architects are perfectly capable of adopting on their own. Every architect who builds in the world soon makes himself capable of thinking in ways other than the one to which he has been acculturated. And every architect of sense will have long ago arrived at an explanation for himself of why this is so, why his design thinking cannot serve as a common currency for transactions with the larger world.

But let me offer here my own explanation for the resistance to design ideas, in the form of a series of observations. I choose these reflections not because they explain the situation comprehensively, but because they lead us to a line of thinking that I hope you will find fruitful (and that is, as you might well guess, the basis for the argument of this book).

It's a much-remarked truism that there is abroad in America just now a pervasive distrust of what might be called empowered expertise—those fields of endeavor that are granted power on the basis of their claim to "know how the world works." It's not hard to see why there might be such distrust. If you were of a certain mind, you could see the whole of our national life since World War II as a parade of "expert professions" being granted power and then either abusing that power or being shown—much too late—not to have known what they were doing. As the list is grudgingly revealed, we are coming to realize that it extends from atomic scientists in the 1940s through liberal bureaucrats in the 1960s to investment bankers in the 1980s. A song lyric from the era of the first revelations sums up our reaction to all that have followed since: we won't get fooled again.

Architecture has its own secure place in this sad litany, stemming from those postwar years when a peculiarly American version of the modernist project was both the national urban policy and the national corporate style. Architecture said that it could provide a diagnosis and prescription for society's ills, and for a while we were granted the power to supply both. The burden that architecture has had to bear in all the years since then is that when we had the power, we blew it. We truly did not know what we were doing, did not foresee the unintended consequences that would flow from what we were proposing.

Since their respective debacles, virtually all of the diagnosing professions have carried out critical, sometimes painful, self-examinations, each recasting itself in an attempt to reestablish its diagnoses as credible to a wary public. Architecture, chastened like all the rest, undertook a recasting of its own project of diagnosis.

I though would like to suggest that this crisis of professionalism stems not so much from actions taken by the stewards of those professions (although plenty are blameworthy); rather, the claim of diagnosis is itself the source of the problem.

If we look at the fields of inquiry that claim to explain the human condition—sociology, religion, politics, psychology, economics, philosophy—none has been able to produce a "metaphysics," a picture of life convincing enough to make us all say, "Yes, that explains why we act as we do and why events happen as they do."

Some of these fields offer insights that are true (sometimes even provably so), but that can be applied only within a strictly defined realm. Economics is an obvious example of such a narrowly applicable field, and so might be politics, and philosophy as it has come to be defined in academia. Others of these fields provide insights that can be applied across the board, but those insights are unprovable. Religion is the prime example here, but we might include as well psychology and sociology.

Because none of the fields of inquiry supply insights that are both comprehensively and provably true, we can feel certitude about any of them only if we can suspend our disbelief. To believe that the ideas of the narrowly true fields explain our lives, we must convince ourselves that the parts of life not covered "don't really matter." To believe in the ideas of the comprehensive but unprovable fields, we must not demand scientific proof for the ideas.

The insights of these fields are thus not universally applicable diagnoses of the human condition. They are limited, either by applicability or verifiability. The problem is that we have no ready categories by which to classify "limited insights into life." What we do have is a yawning pigeonhole entitled "diagnoses of the human condition" that sucks any partial, delimited insight or explanation into its maw. We grab at such partial explanations, hold onto them for what comfort they offer, and try as best we can to blinker ourselves to their shortcomings, in order to garner for ourselves the blessed feeling that the world makes sense.

We are aided in our self-deception by the demands of rhetoric that the explaining professions feel constrained to follow for their own ends, the better to sell their insights in a marketplace of other such insights. An economist's analysis of consumer purchasing patterns never comes with a codicil disclosing the narrowness of its applicability, in terms like "This analysis has no way to account for the effects of these patterns on cultural values." And a psychiatrist seldom actually says that his methods are unverifiable, that they will work only insofar as the patient is convinced of their efficacy. But bereft of these delimiting qualifications, the insights have the look of fitting, like a round peg into a round hole, into that waiting pigeonhole, "diagnoses of the human condition." And so we, eager and unaware, slot them into that category, but once positioned there, they inevitably come to grief, either contradicting each other or being shown up by subsequent events, or when granted actual power, causing us real harm.

Let us agree, for the moment, that architecture, like these other fields of inquiry, is a delimited diagnoser of the human condition. What I want to suggest is that as long as architecture makes *any* claims to diagnosis, no matter how hemmed-in by admitted limitations, it will be sucked into that pigeonhole of universal applicability, and there shown up as not equal to the category, even if the category had never been claimed.

I want to suggest that architecture can escape the crisis of professionalism by carefully claiming to be able to do only that which it actually can do. The bulk of this book will be a search for the shape of such a tenable conception of practice. But for now, we have left a question begging: If architecture's perspective on the human condition is circumscribed, is it limited by applicability or by verifiability?

Actually it's a little of both. See if the following doesn't present the core of architecture's view of the human condition: From our own experience and especially from the example of our design epiphanies, we architects believe that the best life is the reflective life, the life lived so as to exemplify ideas. Those same experiences have convinced us that life is also best when it is lived in harmony with its surroundings. So we believe that the very best condition is when people live in accord with ideas and their surroundings instance those same ideas back to them.

Not an unreasonable philosophy for how to live. There are schools of thought that would offer other visions of The Good Life, but I think it's fair to say that many people would find much to endorse in an ideal of life, ideas and surroundings in concord. The problem comes when we architects take that implicit assent and draw two further conclusions from it—that others could easily live out this concord of ideas and surroundings, and that design ideas are the ones they would choose to live by.

There is a difference between your teacher-inspired epiphany and an architect's design epiphany. While you might yearn for the resolve to live your life so as to enact ideas, architects enact design ideas naturally, as a matter of course. Who but a young architect would be perfectly happy to live in an apartment furnished with only two perfect chairs, so as to have nothing that would not instance design ideas?

But don't for a moment think that I am setting up architects as ethical paragons. We have here not a matter of superior resolution but of natural selection. Architects are people who are sufficiently moved by design ideas to want to live this way. They feel not sacrifice but a positive joy in enacting William Morris's dictum to have nothing around you that you do not know to be useful or believe to be beautiful.

But this very ease of resolution, and the life it can produce, can lead architects unwittingly to a misconception. They forget that for others the resolution to live so as to instance ideas might not come so effortlessly. They forget as well that even for a person with the requisite resolution, the ideas they would resolve to enact might not be *design* ideas. Our imagined teacher, for instance, might explain her world through ideas that are socialist or libertarian or even literary. Concord for her would be surroundings that embodied *those* values.

And they would be forgetting that some people might see the purpose of designed surroundings as being something wholly apart from speaking values. It's quite plausible, for example, to think of a building as a vehicle for bringing about desired *results* in the world—selling clothes, for instance, or educating the young or curing the sick.

So let me state the situation this way. For all of their love of design, for all that design has done for their lives, architects cannot tenably assume that their perspective on buildings speaks for all viewpoints. There are at least two other perspectives on what a building is for. There is the perspective the architect often takes, seeing the building as something that can provide an instance of the *order* that can come from design. But there is also the perspective that sees the building as a way to embody personal or shared *values*. And there is the view that looks to the building to bring about *results*.

These different ways of seeing the building are thus also different reasons for embarking on the design and construction of a building, and different ways of judging whether the completed building has fulfilled the expectations set for it.

The leap I make in this book—and I make it as an architect—is to assert that all three perspectives on the building have an equal claim to having their expectations for the building fulfilled. What I have tried to do in this theory is to find a conception of practice that, while being true to architects' values, gives equal honor to those other two perspectives on what a building is for.

Here is how I will unfold the theory:

My first task in this unfolding is to *distinguish* the three perspectives on the building, by clarifying just what each thinks the building is for. I will do this in two parts. The first part, in chapters 1a and b, will listen in on adherents of the three perspectives talking about the building, on the presumption that we reveal how we think about something by the ways we talk about it in unguarded moments. For this reason, I'll be characterizing the three perspectives on the building as *discourses* about the building—one perspective talking about *order,* one about *values,* and one about *results.*

With the three discourses distinguished one from the other, I will then, in chapters 2a and b, try to give a sense of how the adherents of the two discourses about values and results came to think of the building in the ways they do.

Having performed that task for two of the three discourses, symmetry demands (this *is* a book by an architect, after all) that we perform the same service for the third discourse and examine how architects think. That is the task of chapter 3.

Once we have a handle on how advocates of each of the three discourses think, we need a picture of how they can work together to produce a building that each camp can feel will fulfill its idea of what the building is for. That will be the task of chapter 4.

In that chapter I will construct an idealized model in which each of the two other discourses charges the architect to produce the building that will fulfill its particular conceptions (while the architect simultaneously designs to fulfill the conceptions of her own discourse). What emerges from this discussion is that we already have at hand ways of judging whether a building is likely to fulfill the expectations of both the "order" and "results" conceptions, but we have no such ways of gauging how designs have met the expectations of the "values" discourse. We have no language with which to frame a charge to the architect about values, no way to judge whether a proposed design is likely to produce fulfillment from that "values" perspective, and no standard by which to judge whether fulfillment has actually been achieved in the finished and occupied building.

Chapter 5 sketches a way to fill this void by proposing both a language in which values about living can be addressed alongside ideas about order, and a standard by which to judge when fulfillment of the "values" perspective can be said to have been achieved.

With this, the presentation of the theory is almost complete. I say "almost" because the conception of practice left standing at the end of chapter 5 might look foreign to those fellow architects I encountered at the AIA convention. And that would be a serious fault, for my whole intention in this theory for practice is to not to show that architects "work wrong" in their practices, only that they "think wrong" about how they work—that they labor honorably but do so under theories that force them into untenable claims and judgments, and that those theories are the source of their problems. Chapter 6 makes the case that the vision of practice I present is not only more tenable in its relations with the larger world than the vision of practice currently embraced, but is more attuned to—is indeed derived from—the values by which architects actually live their daily lives.

My sincere hope is that when architects like those at the convention fully grasp the implications of this theory, addressed to them from one who has served a decade in the trenches of practice, they might see at the end of my argumentation not something strange and unattainable but something radically *familiar* to their experience.

1

Other Ways to Think about a Building

1a   Thinking about Results

A question that's not often asked in architecture is: How does it sound to produce a building? What kind of conversation goes on during a building's design, construction, and early occupancy? It's a useful question for us to ask because it is through fairly informal words that we often reveal our deeper values about the things that matter to us. By listening in on some of the words exchanged among architect, client, and contractor, we might be able to get a handle on how each thinks of the building that all are involved with.

If you are an architect from the broad middle of American practice, you will doubtless recognize these snippets of conversation. Perhaps you will remember one or another of them as a cautionary tale from your own experience, or maybe as a hazier (but more telling) story recounted to you from an adjacent bar stool.

"Do we get to do architecture this time?"

Here's a question that a staff designer might ask a senior partner upon her return from the initial meeting with a new client. Significantly, this is not the query, "Will this client accede to everything we propose?" To ask, "Will we do architecture?" is more nearly to ask, "Will design's kind of reasoning have standing in the discussions to follow? Or will the convictions we reach through design be dismissed?"

Just what is "design reasoning"? Numerous books have been written exploring in depth how architects think, but let me propose this formulation. An architect comes to the design task with a repertoire of *paradigms of order.* By that term I mean to convey conceptions as broad as a building-organization schema and as narrow as a favored construction detail. Some of these we draw from architecture's history, some from our own practices. Some paradigms are invented by one architect but then become available to all: think of Le Corbusier's many formal inventions. But for the sake of illustration, let me name one of the most basic ordering paradigms: "two equal spaces on either side of an axis."

With a repertoire of paradigms, including this one, hovering in her head, the architect looks at her client's needs and desires, and tries to find there spaces that can be "made sense of" by composing them in accord with one or another of the paradigms.

"These two needs," she might say to herself, "require spaces of roughly similar size, and the client seems to hold them in similar regard. If I put them on either side of an axis, the client might be able to see and feel in that composition the equivalence of their importance."

Design will explain something about the two rooms ("they are equivalent in importance") and thus make a kind of sense of the activities, the life, to be lived in them. Of course, in a full design this sort of pattern seeking and order matching goes on through higher and higher levels, the order of the building ordering, and inevitably reordering, the smaller orders of the parts. But the principle remains the same: the order of the forms provides an explanation through analogy about the life of the spaces.

When this happens, the architect can feel that she has done architecture. It's every architect's hope that the client will apprehend the order of the forms, sense the analogy they offer about the life of the place, and in that sensing, feel a kind of pleasure. Which is not to say that the architect hopes that her design will pass directly from conception to construction. Other factors must be brought into the mix of considerations: the cost of bringing the concept to reality, the client's personal tastes, the desires of surrounding people and authorities. But those challenges go with the territory; an architect knows that it's possible to insert all these factors into the mix of considerations and still have forms whose order provides an explanation about the life of the place.

No, the question here is not whether architecture can be accomplished, but whether the client will feel enough of that pleasure-by-analogy to accord it value in discussions about the developing design—whether design will have standing.

Architects know that it's most often in buildings meant to make money that design loses its standing. But when this happens, seldom is there an outright expression of dismissal. The modalities are more subtle than that. Here are three of the most common.

• The architect might be pressed to bear what could be called a burden-of-proof of no harm. It's a fact of life that form ordered by design might cost less or more or the same as some putative "form ordered by expedience." Where a form has been ordered by design, a finding of "equal cost" or "less cost" is a happy serendipity. To find, though, that the ordered form costs more requires the client to enter into a rough calculus that weighs the contemplated pleasure of design order against the cost of bringing it into being. But if pleasure-from-design has no standing, it will have no weight with which to counter its costs in the scales of judgment. Here design must prove itself "weightless." It must assure the client that it will be either cost-neutral or actually of benefit in the calculus that does have standing in such a discussion, that of the balance sheet.

• The architect might encounter indifference tempered by indulgence, a position softer than an exclusively bottom-line approach. We can suspect its presence if, after the architect's heartfelt presentation of a design strategy, the client nods distractedly and moves to the next agenda item. Its presence will be confirmed if, after the architect has left the room, one member of the client group recalls the presentation and the client chairman sighs, "Yes, I know, but it's the price you pay when hiring an architect."

• Or the architect might find incomprehension yet exploitation. In this third modality, the architect's presentation might again be recalled to the chairman. This time he might begin his remarks with, "No, I didn't understand what she meant either, but—" and then end with (pick one:) "we need her name on our project" or "it will have great curb appeal" or "it will let us raise our rent structure."

Some of my fellow architects are undoubtedly chuckling at seeing these stock phrases, these old chestnuts of practice, lifted from the province of bar chat and placed into print. But let me bring my colleagues up short. The theme of these scenarios is not "design ideals defeated by venality." Nearer to the truth might be "design ideals offered where not wanted." But both characterizations are flawed in that both leave the architect in sole possession of ideals, and that is a position I want emphatically to reject.

The client in these scenarios plainly sees the building he has commissioned as a mechanism for making a return on his investment and not as a means toward new understandings of living. What is more truly going on here is the mutual incomprehension of two parties operating on different value structures. The architect in these scenarios is acting on the assumption that the client has engaged her to produce form ordered by design. The client's actions flow from his assumption that he has engaged the architect to help him turn a profit.

"But how will that affect the resale value?"

The architect and client are hunched over a set of sketch plans for the client's new house. In the "programming" part of their previous meeting, the client had spoken of her lifelong wish for a secluded place to read. In the "just chatting" interlude that had followed, she had enthused about the tall, object-crammed spaces she had seen in London at John Soane's house-museum, and how the memory of that experience had stayed with her in all the years that followed. Now the architect points, in his new plans, to a tiny room off the stair landing, and he describes how it could be lined with shelves for both books and beloved objects; and how, being at the landing level, it could extend through the height of the second floor all the way to the roof, where there could be a skylight that would stream light over the books and artifacts and—

Lost in his enthusiasm, the architect barely registers the query about resale value when it is uttered; but upon its being repeated, he hears. And in the hearing he begins to harbor the suspicion that, in the design of this house, he will not be doing architecture.

Architects long for the client with unusual desires, unique requirements. Such demands allow for the fullest exercise of those pattern-seeking, order-matching skills that constitute the essence of the architect's art. So it's dismaying to learn that a client doesn't wish for the exercise of those skills. This client, it seems, doesn't conceive of her house as a place that speaks of her unique desires and patterns of living. She has in her mind a conception of how people generally live, and she wishes her house to speak of and accommodate that notion.

Such a desire on the client's part could flow from a variety of motives, the most likely being that she sees the house, at least in part, as an investment. She wants to be certain that she can, at some future date, get out of the house at least the amount of money she has put into it. And to assure that outcome, she believes that her house must be, to some extent, a commodity with broad appeal.

Or perhaps the client's concern for resale is a convenient cover for her reluctance to commit to a house that is "characteristic," quirky, one-of-a-kind. Perhaps she doesn't trust her instincts, fears they might change, feels she can hedge her bets if she goes with the generic. Perhaps, even, she feels more at ease with the already-known, the expected. (Was there never a time, when traveling by car to an unfamiliar locale, when you weren't quite up to engaging "the locals" at the small-town diner, and you went instead to the McDonald's on the bypass? Haven't you sometimes found yourself preferring the no-surprises generality of a Holiday Inn to the "characteristic" local bed-and-breakfast?)

Whatever our client's reasons for preferring the general, we are obliged to concede that those reasons must flow from a structure of values that somehow define what she is. But that concession reveals that our architectural preference for the characteristic likewise flows from a structure of values that defines what we are as architects. What we have in this vignette is not a client who is a robotic captive of the market, nor one lacking in courage, nor one who is out to thwart the accomplishment of architecture. We have a client whose values about home differ from those of her architect.

"Yes, I know it's designed for small shops, but I've got The Gap on the other line!"

Here we have a conflict not between the general and the specific but between order and expedience. The architect has designed an urban office building with a commercial street frontage that can accommodate a number of small shops. He has composed the larger facade of the building on the presumption of a lively proliferation of small-scale elements at its base. In his design he has worked under a social vision of people passing into and spilling out from the many openings of these shops. He has spaced the columns (that extend up several floors) to accommodate a presumed shop width. He has contrived a common service corridor at the rear of the shops to free the public facade of all the accouterments of servicing and waste disposal. Now all of this design thinking must be rethought.

It's not so much the matter of the time and money he'll have to spend to do this rethinking (he has written his contract to cover circumstances like these). It's not even really the client's cavalier presumption that he can easily accommodate this last-minute change. It is the certain knowledge that the building will not now be as consistent, not as ordered, not as *good* as it could have been.

Our architect had, after countless false starts, conceived a design idea rich enough that its logical entailments could accommodate every aspect of the building program as it had been presented to him. He had found that the sub-ideas of that conception had almost "told" him how to deploy the structure, the mechanical systems, the movement of people, the composition of the facades. His conviction about his design concept had only grown as the design developed: for every new condition that arose, his concept had seemed able to tell him how to handle it.

Until now. Too late to rethink the design from scratch; he would have to patch it up as best he could. And of course he would do it.

But he would know that the difficulty of doing so would never be perceived or appreciated. And the resulting fall from order would never be adequately mourned, never be appreciated in its full meaning except by himself and his staff.

It's just about the saddest story an architect can tell. Excellence turned into expedience, and without even an acknowledgement of the dimensions of what has happened. But even here the situation is one of values in disjuncture. The reason-for-being of the commercial space at the base of the building had been its ability to generate rental income. If more income, or more dependable income, could be gotten by renting out those spaces to one big retailer, then that is what must happen. The value system of commercial development has no way of thinking about, much less weighing, what architects call order. If we architects choose to make design order out of what commerce provides to us, then we must acknowledge that we do that order-making for our own motives, for the excellence it can garner under our own value structure. To expect honor for that effort from those not subscribing to our values is to expect in vain.

"But you said your budget was—"

After a long and ultimately futile effort by the architect to produce a design that might be built within the prescribed budget, the client admits that she can spend, after all, just a little more.

Here is a scenario that looks like naked duplicity. But even this is more truly a misunderstanding of values in disjuncture. The client has learned, in experiencing life through her value structure, that the price of everything is subject to negotiation, and that the way to win a negotiation is to begin the bidding with a "lowball" offer. The architect, though, has taken the client's budget figure and put it in the same conceptual bowl with her specifications about the number of bedrooms she requires in her house or the preferred manner of receiving patients in her clinic.

The client, by the dictates of her value structure, has conceived a great divide between her "needs" (which she states truly) and her "resources" (which she lowballs). The architect, however, has seen no such divide, has seen all the client's pronouncements as the ground upon which he is charged to operate.

Our architect may feel unfairly deceived, but the truth of the matter is that the client was playing one kind of game while the architect was playing another. The deception was not in the game the client played. It was in her not announcing its name and nature.

What the client in this scenario doesn't sufficiently appreciate, though, are the consequences of her actions for the design of the building. She imagines, out of her values, that the architect will now, in the face of this change, merely put back into the design those things he had been forced to excise under the pressure of her negotiating stance. Her lowballing, she believes, will have squeezed out the superfluous, forced the architect to prioritize. But the architect knows that the design order possible in "The Game of $250,000" is not merely more of the order possible under "The Game of $200,000." It is likely to be an order quite different. But to seek that other order now, to play this newly declared game from scratch, is impossible. There's not enough time left on the clock.

"We want to substitute this sink for the one you specified."

The building has finally passed into construction, and the contractor wants to install a brand of lavatory different from the one the architect had chosen for the many bathrooms in the client's proposed clinic. Every architect knows the bother such a substitution entails: a whole train of design decisions must be unearthed and rethought. How will the look of this new sink accord with the counter tops designed for another kind of sink? How will this new sink go with the soap and towel dispensers, chosen to have their own design accord with the light fixtures? Will the new sink's different dimensions make the rows of basins too cramped or too loose? Will it accommodate the specified drains and faucets? And on and on. And these are the considerations for a relatively small item, one without too much ramification for the whole design. For a truly major substitution, the re-evaluation time can increase exponentially.

Are all these difficulties merely another case of two parties operating out of different value structures? Yes they are. Under the contractor's values, "the difference of a dollar" is a sufficient basis for changing a decision. Granted, in some cases a "bother" factor ("That's more trouble than it's worth") could act to impede such a change. But in truly market-driven institutions (like large contractors and commercial clients), there will be staff people sitting around on payroll whose job is to find such small savings. Far from being a bother, finding that "difference of a dollar" justifies the cost of their wages. Not just a philosophical orientation but an institutional momentum drives such efforts. Once a savings is found, the decision of what action to take is automatic, effortless.

But the decision that's automatic for the contractor's value structure is, for the architect's values, a matter of great complexity and effort. For her, the difference of a dollar is far from sufficient to tell her what to do. To make her decision she must go back to her plans, undo and reknit a whole train of interconnected design decisions, and see if the new configuration is as consistent and ordered as the old one had been—and if it is not, to decide somehow how much the diminution is worth in dollars. And she must do this all the while knowing, if she is alert to such things, that only under her value structure has a diminution occurred at all.

"The building didn't get us more clients (make us more efficient, communicative, innovative . . .)."

No, it didn't, and who told you that it would? Surely your architect had more sense than to promise you that directly. More likely it was one of those presumptions that never got voiced and so never required direct refutation. But where did the presumption come from in the first place?

One source might have been the American Institute of Architects itself, either through its *Manual of Practice* or through advertisements it has placed, from time to time, in big-business magazines. Not that the AIA ever makes explicit guarantees in its ads (not even headache remedies do that). Its strategy for promoting architecture in such ads is to offer services that business will find useful: "In hiring an architect you will have a single point of coordination for your project." "An architect can help you organize and prioritize your needs." But the subtext of these messages is that architecture will be good for your business.

It is plainly true that architects do perform the kinds of services the AIA touts, services with direct, measurable benefit to business. We architects do facilities analysis, maintenance projections, user-needs studies, programming, cost breakdowns, construction coordination—we do all this and more, gladly. The problem is that these services don't really call on us to use the skills and beliefs that define us as architects, those design skills of pattern finding, order matching and order coordinating. To promote business-friendly skills as the reason to hire an architect is like saying, "Go to a physician: you'll have all your medical records kept in one convenient place."

Here's the quandary: The services that business finds useful are, to architects, peripheral. And the service that is central to architecture—ordering space to ideas about living—is of no measurable benefit to commerce.

The rub of course is that commerce holds all the cards. Its values determine what may legitimately be said, which arguments will have force. Imagine a scene in a corporate boardroom. One of the members says, "We shouldn't do X because that will reduce our profit by ten percent." Now imagine another member saying, "We shouldn't do X because that will disrupt the regular column grid." The inadmissability of the second argument, in that context, is obvious.

The important point to take from this is not that the column-grid argument is invalid, only that it has no *standing*, no force in that context. In a different context, say a design school studio, the argument about profitability would be the one that lacked standing. Considerations of regularity would carry the day.

The reason that design values so often look to be on the short end of a power hierarchy is due to the number and importance of the contexts in which commercial values set the agenda. In those contexts, design's values, in themselves equivalent to those of commerce, are rendered marginal by the superior power associated with commercial values. In and of themselves, design values and market values are only values in disjunction. It is contingent circumstance that puts them in a power hierarchy.

If we begin from that understanding, and discount the power hierarchy, we might be able to imagine a theoretical structure that encompasses both design values and business values. The first step is to *distinguish* the two, admit right up front that design values do not encompass commercial values, nor are they coextensive with them. The two value structures are distinct, and any attempt to reconcile them will only result in the distortion of one or the other.

Step two in in our theorizing about value structures would be to *characterize* them, set out what each believes, where those beliefs come from, and how each system of belief operates. Having done that, step three would be to *relate* them, to describe the manner in which the different value structures could transact with each other. Describing that relationship is the work of later chapters, but the tasks of distinguishing and characterizing can begin here.

The common ground of the two value structures—the reason they are engaged at all—is the building under design. If they are talking past each other, the building is the thing they are talking past each other about. And the reason the two discussions don't connect is that each is talking about the building as a different thing.

Our Soane-inspired client saw her home, at least in part, as either a commodity she could sell for a profit or as a way to hedge her bets about how to expend her resources. Our commercial clients saw the building as a way to generate income, through renting it out or by using it as an integral part of a mechanism for creating products or services that could be sold. Our contractor saw the building as a way to keep his staff profitably busy, but primarily as the very means by which to conduct his chosen business.

All of them saw the building as something they could use to accomplish a purpose apart from bringing the building into existence. They saw the building, and spoke of it, as an *effectuator of anticipated results*. By contrast, our designers saw the building as a medium by which ideas could be made apprehensible through paradigms of architectural order. They saw the building, and talked about it, as an *instantiator of order.*

That's the basis from which each party talked, but to discuss propositions about the building (which is what design conversation must be) requires that each party have a way to evaluate propositions presented by the other party: "Is that proposed possibility, by my lights, a good or bad thing?"

When our clients and contractor looked at the results that alternative building designs might bring them, they gauged those results by their anticipated monetary consequences (the more money, the better). Our architects judged alternative designs on a scale of consistency, of how well the design's orders accorded with each other.

This, then, is how each of the parties framed their talking: Each was saying those things that proceeded from their conception of what the building was for, and each was advocating those alternatives that would result in gains, as measured by the value systems each held. Let us call such advocacy talk a *discourse.*

We've just seen a discourse about *results* and a discourse about *order.* Let me now have you listen in on more talk, to uncover another way of thinking about the building, another discourse.

1b   Thinking about Values

Listen again to the sound of a building being designed:

"We've got to educate the client."

This is sometimes the strategy that's advocated when the goal of the client is discovered to be something other than architecture. In such a case the "education" is a matter of selling the client on the idea that there can be pleasure in a building's order explaining about the life lived there, in effect educating the client about what architecture is and what it can do. But more often this phrase has a simpler import, which can be stated as: "We've got to educate the client's taste." We've got to bring her to like the kinds of things we like.

"Taste" is one of those terms (like "beauty") that has dropped almost completely out of the architect's lexicon. Once a hot topic in artistic circles, succeeding redefinitions of taste over the past couple of centuries have so canceled each other out that the term has come to seem meaningless. Try to explain, rigorously, what it means to say, "He has taste." But change that sentence to "He has *tastes,*" and sense begins to peek through. Clearly this means that he has preferences, and in terms of architecture, preferences about how things look and feel.

Why does someone come to have such preferences? We might say that we prefer something—say, a chair—when its look and feel give us pleasure. What, then, is the source of the pleasure? Here we might say that pleasure comes when we feel a connection between a certain kind of chair and something in our lives that we value or desire. That *something* could be the memory of a chair with similar qualities, a belief that a chair like that will associate us with a desired lifestyle, even a long-held curiosity about what it would be like to sit in such a chair. But whatever the *something* is, that chair, when it has the right look and feel, *speaks that* to us in ways that merely imagining the *something* never could.

Extend this idea outward from the chair to the room to the building, and we can see that to have preferences in architecture is to feel that certain ways of looking and feeling embody your desires and values, while other ways do not.

So this scenario of educating the client is not really a matter of the deep probity of the architect's design methods versus the mere caprice of the client. It's more truly a matter of two belief systems contesting for the same ground. Both the architect and the client have ideas about how forms might embody values. The architect who wants to educate the client implicitly regards the client's values as invalid.

And it's not just the client who has such ideas.

"Yes, but my brother (my cousin the plumbing contractor, my lawyer, my decorator) said that I should . . . "

The architect begins proposing design solutions to the client, and other voices are invoked in the discussion. Some of the voices (like that of the brother) might speak from much the same perspective as the client herself. Others might view the enterprise of designing and building as having an entirely different purpose (in the lawyer's case, as a matter of estate planning or liability exposure). Others (like the plumber) might have a different perspective on prioritizing costs. And still others (like the decorator) might have an alternative philosophy about design itself.

Every architect knows this phenomenon of additional cooks hovering over the broth as it simmers, and it's easy to understand why an architect would prefer to be the sole chef for the design. One reason is operational. No one likes to be second-guessed when he works: it can both bog down progress and muddy the result.

A second reason is professional. Anyone who is hired for his judgment resents having that judgment questioned. It's not solely a matter of ego or turf defense. There will always arise situations in which a professional has to make decisions for the client that are judgment calls, best guesses informed by his experience. A professional can do that only if the client gives him the benefit of the doubt, and trusts his judgment above that of others.

The third reason, though, is specific to architects. If the architect in his preliminary designs has begun to find paradigms of order that match patterns in the client's life, he will have come to feel conviction about those paradigms. Their orderliness and consistency might even tempt him to the belief that their explanation-of-life is comprehensive, that the ideas of those other participants are either encompassed within his designed order or rendered superfluous by it.

But look at the matter from the other side, from the point of view of the kibitzers hovering around the simmering pot. Are they actually trying to do the architect's job?

Look first at what they're not doing. They are not proposing alternative ways to size beams or ducts, nor are they disputing whether building code requirements have been met. They are not interested in having input into the fact-based, objective aspects of the design. They are concerned with judgmental, value-laden questions.

What they truly want is not to do the design themselves but to see their values embodied in the design the architect does. But they've been brought into the discussion when design is going on; and when design is happening, only matters of design can be talked about. The modalities of the situation cause them to couch their "values" thoughts in "design" terms. The client's lawyer might be thinking, "I hope she'll consider the risks of liability in this building of hers," but the situation makes that thought come out as, "I think you ought to beef up that railing there."

We've all encountered situations of this kind, in committees and in personal discussions, where the manner in which a topic is being treated has the effect of conditioning how we express ourselves.

Often we're not even aware of how we're tailoring our comments to the context, realizing what we have done only afterward with thoughts like "Why on earth did I say that?"

But it's not just the unconscious conforming-to-the-admissible that turns values input into design rivalry. There is also the resentment that comes from seeing your input, no matter how couched, first excluded and then discounted. Exacerbating the situation is that present-day climate of suspicion of authority mentioned earlier. After twenty years of cover-up and stonewalling, we hear the simple statement "My best judgment is . . . " and to our minds leap, unbidden, thoughts like "Who is she to say that?" and "What's he hiding anyway?"

So we could argue from a purely operational standpoint that the architect ought, right from the start, to hear the thoughts of all those people who have the client's ear. They'll make their thoughts known sooner or later: best to get them on board early.

But there's a more substantive, and less self-serving, reason for doing this. To the extent that those other people do have the client's ear, to that extent their ideas constitute an integral part of her *universe of desires and values,* out of which the architect will draw the patterns that form the basis for his design. To work without those other ideas is to work from a diminished basis. And as we have seen before, when the basis of design is diminished, the patterns aren't just "lesser," they are likely to be materially different.

So it's not just in the architect's interest but in the interest of the design itself that the universe of desires and values be stated as comprehensively as can be managed. Look now, though, at two situations in which this imperative for comprehensiveness is thwarted.

"We'd better shoot the photographs quickly."

Shoot them, that is, before the client's patterns of living start to generate artifacts that compromise the consistency of the design.

It is the great cliché and open secret of architectural photography that the camera prefers images in which every visible feature seems of a piece with the perceived effect of the whole: the eye takes in the theme of the total picture and then, as it sweeps the image for detail, finds that every incident contributes, consistently, to that theme. And what the camera likes, the journals will like even more.

Charles Moore, when pressed, would sheepishly tell the story of how Moore Lyndon Turnbull Whittaker's houses of the early 1960s were photographed for publication. *Sunset* magazine had by then become the purveyor-to-millions of the California Lifestyle, and Charles was determined to position his houses to ride that wave. They would be made the very image of California life and thus irresistible to *Sunset's* editors. And so, at the completion of an MLTW house, the architects would present the owners with a surprise gift—a weekend at some scenic spot "so as not to bother you while the house is being shot." Immediately upon the owners' departure, up would pull the architects with a truckload of furniture, accessories, even wall paint; and not far behind them, the photographers. After a frenzy of undoing and redoing, the unsuspecting owners would return, and a few months later, open *Sunset* to find their house in a lavish spread—but furnished in the photos with Mexican *equipales* chairs, kachina dolls, and Navaho rugs. Few seemed to notice that they were the same chairs, dolls, and rugs that had appeared in all the previous *Sunset* spreads of MLTW houses. But thus does an architect hitch his wagon to a star, and in fact become one.

Charles Moore told the story sheepishly because in actuality he greedily seized upon the funky inconsistencies of his clients' ways of living as grist for his design mill. He recognized those *Sunset* images for what they were: marketing tools. But other architects, with a less ecumenical perspective, are sometimes seduced by the ordered consistency of the not-yet-lived-in house and its recorded image, and come to believe that *that* is the truth of design.

But what such a belief betrays is that the design never embodied the full range of the client's desires and values in the first place. Rather, the design picked and chose only those patterns that could be matched to a narrow range of ordering paradigms, those that made up the architect's "style." Patterns that couldn't be matched up were set aside, either overtly through a flourish of rhetoric, or covertly in hopes that they wouldn't be missed. But desires and values can't be wished away; we will feel their absence, and to compensate for that absence we will make settings where we can feel their presence. If the client longs for a cozy nook for reading, a floor lamp and an overstuffed chair will find their way into the tall white living room the architect has provided. If your client's conception of coziness is not part of your design vision, then you'd better shoot those photographs quickly, before that, and much else, happens.

"You do as you think best. We'll move in when we return from Europe."

Here is the converse of the architect diminishing the universe of desires and values to achieve her style: the clients abdicating their desires and values to achieve the architect's style.

What's wrong with this? Nothing at all, if the clients truly know what they are authorizing. What an architect does in such a situation (all an architect can do in such a situation) is to take whatever sketchy desires the client has communicated, along with the facts of the site, and then from the paradigms of order that match parts of those patterns, choose those that are characteristic of her oeuvre. The development of the design then consists primarily of the chosen paradigms "working their will," in much the same way that chosen musical themes do in the variations of Bach or Mozart. As with a work of variations, the pleasure of the design comes from our knowing the conventions of order associated with the paradigms and then sensing how they have been manipulated.

Stated that way, the whole matter sounds dreadfully arcane. But we don't have to be able to retrace an architect's every move in a design to be moved by what she has done. After all, we don't have to know all the conventions of Baroque musical composition to enjoy the Goldberg Variations. All that is really required is that we be of a mind that accepts the idea of conventional rules and feels a delight in seeing them skillfully and creatively played out.

If the client has given truly informed consent to having a house whose pleasures are of that kind, then none of my strictures about a comprehensive universe of desires and values apply. Such a house is being designed for a purpose different from the embodiment of values. It is being designed to instance order.

"The maintenance staff has made a few changes . . ."

Every architect knows this situation. (It's another reason for shooting the photographs quickly.) We may think we put our building in the hands the owner, but in actually we commend it into the grip of the maintenance staff. As the building's fittings wear out, as new needs arise, does anyone think to phone the architect for advice on how to make the required changes accord with the building already in place? Oh, no. The call goes down to the maintenance shop to "work something up."

Even important buildings are not immune to this proclivity. Boston's new Back Bay train station has gotten the janitorial treatment, despite the fact that it was intended as a civic monument and is appreciated as such by nearly everyone in town, and despite the fact that the offices of its architects are all of four blocks away. Electrical conduit has begun to snake over its carefully detailed concrete surfaces, in the service of additional speakers and security lighting. The brushed stainless steel door handles, so good in the hand, have undergone the inevitable vandalizing, but how have they been replaced? In some cases with one-by-fours on bushings, and in others by door-pulls from the local Ace Hardware.

I describe these changes not to rouse indignation over the desecration of a fine building, and not to have you throw up your hands at the powerlessness of architects, and least of all to show up the staff of the transportation authority as insensitive boors. No, my purpose is to return our attention to that universe of desires and values and the paradigms of order that can be drawn from it.

We saw earlier how people with an interest in a building can find their input ruled inadmissible into that universe of values. Here is another instance of that exclusion, and the visible consequences. Whatever the precise circumstances of the design of Back Bay station, we know from experience that the input of certain groups is often "marginalized" in the design process for a large building, either by outright exclusion or by a more subtle devaluation or discounting of their views. The presumption is often that Management, which has shown skill in organizing such people for efficient production, will also know "what's best for them" in matters of design. Much has been written in condemnation of such an attitude, and many organizations have taken great strides in democratizing the design process—often out of a sincere desire for fairness, sometimes out of a hope for efficiency-enhancing design on the model of "quality circles" in enlightened manufacturing. I, though, want to approach the issue of worker involvement from the standpoint of the needs of design itself.

My first point merely expands a contention made earlier, that when the universe of desires and values is not comprehensive, it renders defective the patterns from which the architect draws paradigms of order. My second point reaffirms another earlier contention, that when people feel their input excluded by Authority, they feel a sense of resentment, at Authority and all its works. When this happens, even design that might otherwise be esteemed comes to be resented. And architects above all others ought to know why: in their very form such works embody "exclusion" and the Management values that caused it. The door pull that might otherwise be liked for its strength and well-machined connections comes to speak, to the maintenance worker—in precisely the way that architecture speaks—not of its inherent qualities but of Management and all the values Management has displayed to him in all the years he has worked there.

Given the manner in which so many companies are run these days, it's little wonder that people in marginalized groups might feel resentment toward the design that Management gives them. And worse for us architects: the more "designed" something appears to be, the more explicitly it displays itself as a product of Management. And even more: to the extent that workers see Management as complicit with the moneyed class that talks on cellular phones in their BMWs, the architect-designed door-pull will speak *that* to them as well.

But it's not just class conflict that drives this resentment. Alasdair MacIntyre (from whom you will hear more in the next chapter) points out that it's a condition of life that every person seeks to achieve his or her own plans in the world, and to do this each of us tries to render predictable as much of the world as we can. But complementarily, to keep ourselves from being pawns in someone else's plans, each of us seeks to be opaque to others, our actions unpredictable.[1] It's one of those existential balancing acts we have to manage if we are to live among other people: to advance our own ends, we try to predict how others will act while trying to thwart their predictions about us.

But management as a practice attempts to tilt the balance all in its favor. What the "science" of management asserts is that it can name those actions or policies which will produce a describable pattern of behavior in employees[2]—making them, in effect, pawns in its plans, able to predict what they will do while keeping its own actions opaque to their knowledge. Who wouldn't resent the unfairness, the presumption of such a set-up?

Architecture is thus doubly burdened when it designs for Authority. By the very nature of who pays for what we design we are inescapably entwined with the people and groups in power. To the extent that those in authority manage their staffs along the lines just described, those people will view us architects and our works as complicit in a resented system. That much we can't escape. (Who among us can afford to refuse a commission over the fine points of a client's personnel policy?) What we can escape though is the further resentment we bring on ourselves when we conduct our design work along those "management science" lines. Do I need to point out the similarities between business management's claim as unseen predictor of behavior and architecture's claim as true diagnoser of the human condition? Here is yet another reason for us architects to reject the idea that through design values alone we can know what people need and how they would wish to act.

These vignettes shows that it's in our interest as architects to avoid the assumption that "we know best" and instead to seek out and hear the desires and values of marginalized groups and include them in our design work. It's in the interest of our designs and how they will be read. It's in the interest of our buildings and how they will be handled. And it's in the interest of our profession and how it will be perceived by the larger public.

There are voices beyond those of the staff that ask to have their values heard, and yet more reasons for hearing them.

"It looks like a jail (a whorehouse, a collision of boxcars . . .)."

Our universe of desires and values needs the input of one more group, the larger public. And it's needed for the same reasons we needed the input of the client's brother and the maintenance staff—to achieve a comprehensive basis from which to design, to forestall resentment over exclusion, and to provide the grounds for engendering trust through design.

It is the failure to build trust that most often occasions comments like those voiced above. I will grant that sometimes a design might indeed look like a jail, in which case the architect ought to do some reality-checking on his perceptions. But often such characterizations are more truly an in-your-face way of saying "I don't understand why it looks like that." The architect of course knows why it looks like that: it's his version of a paradigm of order that orchestrates all the other smaller paradigms drawn from the life of the place. If in his programming work he has opened himself to the input of all concerned, and if he has truly sought to embody those concerns in his design, then he'll have established the basis from which he can explain, to any who might ask, why the building is the way it is. They might reject his thinking (in which case he might decide to do some reworking), but they just might say, "Oh, yes; now I can see how that makes sense."

Time was when it might have been difficult to find a forum in which to hear the public's concerns about a building proposal and their later reaction to its design. No more. The world in which an architect works today is organized and empowered, into both officially constituted review boards and self-appointed interest groups, all of whom are more than willing, and able, to tell what's on their minds.

Almost every architect has his own memory of the Public Hearing from Hell, and it's true that some interest groups exist merely to prevent anything from being built. But let's ignore them in this discussion (even if we can't ignore them in life) and focus on people with a sincere interest in the building being contemplated.

What is the character of what they are saying when they talk about the building's materials, its height, the trash and noise it will generate, "the crowd it will attract"? I would suggest that they are speaking about the building as an *embodier of values*. And as such they are speaking in the same discourse as were the client, the client's cousin and lawyer, and the maintenance staff. All have a legitimate interest in the design of the building. All want to see their values recognized and embodied in it because that is what they see the building as *being for*. They are thinking and talking of the building in a discourse about *values*.

There is an interesting parallel here, at the end of this section, to the discussion that ended the last section. There we saw that when the discourse about order got mixed up with the discourse about results, order got distorted. Here we've just seen how values can be distorted when they get mixed up with order.

When the discourses aren't distinguished, when they are confounded with each other, when they are applied in inappropriate contexts, a sort of "Paper-Scissors-Stone" game takes place. You recall the game: stone breaks scissors, scissors cut paper, paper covers stone. It's a game of trumps. In this chapter we have seen how, when the discourses breach the boundaries of their different perspectives and get into the same game, "results" can trump "order" by its power. We know as architects how "order," by its very orderliness, can appear to trump the messy, unresolved values of a client group. The deep belief of this theory for practice is that when the interests of any one discourse are trumped by another, all will lose in some measure. But if you can keep the discourses separate, pay each its due, and operate under its rules, then all interests will win.

2

Getting Specific about Other Ways of Thinking

2a   From Results to the Market

If it now takes three discourses to talk comprehensively about a building, was there ever a time when a single way of thinking could encompass all that could be thought about a building? And if there was such a time, how did thinking about buildings change between then and now?

I want to suggest that there was such a time, and that a change has taken place between then and now. I will not purport, though, to explain or even trace the change. Such a true history would require an author with talents vastly different from mine. I want instead merely to illustrate the nature of the change, and to do that by dropping us down lightly at a few particularly telling points in time.

Our initial landing spot is Florence, where the first and greatest treatise on architecture has just been published.

freeze-frame:

Alberti's *De re aedificatoria*, 1486

Leon Battista Alberti's *On the Art of Building* certainly purports to cover all that can be thought about the subject, so let's take the great man at his word and look at how he conceived the art of designing, building, and occupying architecture. To read Alberti in the present moment, though, is to experience the feeling described by Michel Foucault, in the famous prefatory passage to his *The Order of Things,* upon his reading a story by Jorge Luis Borges. In that story Borges told of an encounter with a "certain Chinese encyclopedia" in which animals were categorized as:

a) belonging to the Emperor, b) embalmed, c) tame, d) suckling pigs, e) sirens, f) fabulous, g) stray dogs, h) included in the present classification, i) frenzied, j) innumerable, k) drawn with a very fine camelhair brush, l) et cetera, m) having just broken the water pitcher, n) that from a long way off look like flies.

Foucault's reaction, which surely parallels our own, is to note "the stark impossibility of thinking *that*."[1]

Foucault uses this literary example to illustrate his concept of the *epistème.* Each era has its own particular way of making sense of reality, its own *epistème,* and these ways change over time, to the extent that what was sensible to one era comes to seem incomprehensible to other eras.

Reading Alberti evokes a similar feeling of *strangeness,* of the incomprehensibility of thinking what he thinks. Take for example not the content but the organizational logic implicit in the final book of *On the Art of Building,* ostensibly about the restoration of stuctures:

Since we are talking about restoring buildings, we need to inquire into what causes buildings to deteriorate, one of those causes being water. That being so, I will talk about water in its various forms—swamps, water supplies, wells, springs, cisterns, the planting and irrigation of vines, rivers . . . Now, rivers are used to transport goods and so are roads and canals, so I will talk for a moment about the construction of highways and the digging of canals. And since a prime concern with canals is the maintenance of their banks, I will talk about the seashore, which like a canal-bank, is a meeting of water and land . . .

Try thinking *that*. But it's altogether fitting that Alberti's reasoning would seem strange to us. He was reasoning out of an *epistème* different from ours—which is presisely what we are seeking after all, a conception of the art of building different from our own.

Absolutely essential to that conception was an idea I'd like us to call *virtù.* I use the term in the Italian because the moral freight of the usual English translation, virtue, would mislead our understanding. Using *virtù* also keeps the *strangeness* of the concept before us, and evokes as well some of the qualities still esteemed in some circles of Italian society: dignity, self-possession, conducting and displaying one's self in accord with one's station, deference to one's betters, patronage to one's inferiors, etc.

But if those qualities of *virtù* have survived into the present day (have indeed come to define the cliché of an Italian man of a certain age), the moral framework that gave them meaning has not. Alasdair MacIntyre describes that framework in his fittingly titled book *After Virtue.*

MacIntyre is careful to point out that at any moment in time there are likely to be competing moral frameworks, some ascending in dominance, some diminishing, some held by only a small elite but nonetheless influential. MacIntyre describes in great detail the ethical system held in the humanist circles that would likely have included Alberti in their number. Ethics, to those people, was a straightforward matter. From daily experience we know the condition of "man-as-he-happens-to-be." Ancient wisdom describes for us "man-as-he-could-be-if-he-realized-his-essential-nature"—man's *telos.* Ethics are simply those acts that will move us from the first condition to the second.[2] To know your essential nature, your *telos,* to accept it and do those acts that will move you toward it—that is *virtù.*

So when Alberti sets out the following description of the architect, he is not (as we would assume under our way of thinking) engaged in boasting. He is describing his *telos,* the essential nature toward which he aspires.

To conclude, then, let it be said that the security, dignity, and honor of the republic depend greatly on the architect: it is he who is responsible for our delight, entertainment, and health while at leisure, and our profit and advantage while at work, and in short, that we live in a dignified manner, free from any danger. In view then of the delight and wonderful grace of his works, and of how indispensable they have proved, and in view of the benefit and convenience of his inventions, and their service to posterity, he should no doubt be accorded praise and respect, and be counted among those most deserving of mankind's honor and recognition.[3]

He is saying, "This is the *telos* of the architect. Because I profess to be an architect, you may judge me in this way: if I act so as to approach this standard, then I will have displayed *virtù.*"

It was vital to Alberti that this *telos* and its implied acts of *virtù* be established in the minds of his time, for to be without a *telos*, to be without a known nature, was unthinkable. Florentine society had no universal standards of conduct that applied to everyone. The only way to judge whether a person was acting properly was by reference to his *telos*, his role in society. Certain acts constituted *virtù* for a banker, other acts were proper for an artisan. And not just acts but styles of dress, modes of speech, and (vitally for us) types of house were considered appropriate ways to approach nearer to the *telos* of your role.

For the role of magistrate, for example, Alberti declares that

The family home should correspond to the character on whom he has modeled his life, whether king, tyrant, or private citizen. There are certain buildings most suitable to this class of person.[4]

What would be the nature of a house suitable for the class of person with the role of magistrate? Here it's important to realize that in Alberti's Florence, not just people but also things have a *telos*. As MacIntyre puts it, "every type of item which it is appropriate to call good or bad—including persons and actions [and buildings]—has, as a matter of fact, some given specific purpose or function."[5] It is by reference to the given purpose of the thing that one can factually decide whether it is good or bad, whether it is suitable or not.

So when Alberti says that "houses for people in such positions ought to contain a spacious reception area and a route out into the forum, wide enough not to be blocked by the retinue of domestic servants, clients, bodyguards, and others crowding around in their eagerness to accompany them,"[6] he is not saying, "This sort of thing often happens to people of rank, so you'd better provide for it." He is saying that this is what the life of a magistrate in a society of deference and patronage should be like, this is *virtù* for such a man. So a house that provides the settings for that life will be, by definition, suitable for a man of that station. His architect will feel it suitable, the patron will feel it suitable, so indeed will all of Florentine society.

So there was no need for a discussion, in Alberti's time, about what values a building ought to embody. Once you specified the patron's station in society, everyone in Florence would know the values proper for such a person. The only conceivable house or place of business suitable for such a person would be one that embodied those values.

But if a separate "values" discourse did not yet exist, what about thinking of the building as an effectuator of results? When you built in Alberti's time, what result did you expect to bring about? A commodious home for your family, a place to enact the ceremonies expected of you, a place soundly built—all that goes without saying. Alberti, though, gives away a prime motive when he says, almost offhandedly, "Anyone who builds so as to be praised for it—as anyone with good sense would . . ."[7]

Now "praise" is one of those words whose import has changed since Alberti's time. It's not as if our home builder is anticipating the moment when the scaffolding is dismantled and all his friends come up to him in the piazza and say, "Nice *house*, Lorenzo!"

"Praise," to a Florentine, was tied up with the concept of *virtù*, of living so as to approach nearer to the *telos* of your station in life. So "praise*worthy*" is closer to Alberti's meaning, the certain knowledge that you have done the right thing, brought yourself nearer to your essential nature, and thus earned for yourself (in the eyes of your fellow Florentines, who are all the people who matter) *virtù*. When you build seriously, that is the result you seek.[8]

In the times before Alberti, it was assumed that *virtù* would be yours if the building ennobled your ceremonies by its layout, provided the comforts you needed, and was built soundly. Alberti's signal achievement was to convince his time, and all the times thereafter, that this was not enough: both the layout of the rooms and the manner of building had to be disciplined by *order*.

We need not go into the details of Alberti's arguments for this position (they have been covered in many other places and have, in any case, much of that *strangeness* about them), but rather note his conclusions and the manner in which he advocates for them.

Alberti's conclusions are the single thing for which his treatise is best known—a series of prescriptions on the composition of buildings and the proportioning of their rooms. In his book he presents us with woodcuts and word-pictures of schematic building plans, building elevations, and ideal room shapes, all regulated by a system of whole-number ratios. But why were these ideas convincing to the mind of his time?

MacIntyre's *telos* might give us a clue. The *good thing* is the thing that moves from "as it happens to be" toward "how it could be if it realized its essential nature." What else was Alberti doing, in presenting his regulating number system, but revealing the essential nature of building? To build this way is to draw nearer to the *telos* of building. If "drawing nearer to your *telos*" is the standard by which you conduct your life, then surely the building that embodies your *telos* should be designed to a similar standard. It should aspire to its *telos* as you do to yours.

With this argument, the concerns voiced in our three discourses are unified in a single conception. The values to be embodied in a building are known and accepted by all. It is to evince participation in those values that we build seriously. And the proper means to make those values visible is ideal geometric order.

Not, obviously, the way we conceive the building enterprise today. To illustrate how our conception has changed since then, I want to take us down two paths. On the first path we will look at changes in the way a building was to *accomplish things,* and in that way see how the idea developed of speaking of a building as an effectuator of results. The second path will deal with the question of *whose needs were accommodated and how;* the answers to that question will show us the rise of the idea of speaking of a building as an embodier of values.

freeze-frame:

Ledoux's Saltworks of Chaux, 1778

Here is a building complex with an explicit task to accomplish, the manufacture of salt for the Franche-Comté region of France. The process of making salt in the eighteenth century was straightforward. Salt water from a spring was piped (in the case of Chaux, for a number of miles) to a saltworks, where it was evaporated in big flat pans heated by wood fires. After about two days, the brine was reduced to a sort of salt mush, which was then scooped out and spread on drying racks. Once dry, the salt crystals were packed into barrels and carried away by horse-cart.[9]

Simple enough, but now look at the building complex devised by Claude-Nicolas Ledoux to house the process. It is in effect a "company town," with living quarters for the workers and officials as well as the factory itself. At the bottom of the great semicircle of the complex is the gatehouse, through which all materials and people would have to pass. It contains the expected spaces for dispatchers but, as well, a guardhouse, courtroom and jail cells, and a bakery. In the arc to the left of the gatehouse is the pavilion where the barrel makers both lived and worked, and to the right, a matching building for the blacksmiths who would make, among other things, the hoops for the barrels. Completing the semicircle are the two pavilions that contain the living quarters of the salt workers.

At the center of the chord of the semicircle stands the building for the director of the saltworks. By far the tallest and most imposing structure in the complex, it contains the director's living quarters,

Royal Saltworks at Chaux, overall view (upper semicircle not built)

apartments for visiting officials, and a chapel. To the left and right of the director's building are the big barnlike structures where the salt is produced, and beyond them, left and right, houses for the overseers of the operation. Finally, extending outward from the semicircle of buildings to the wall-and-ditch enclosing the complex, are gardens for the workers, the overseers, and the director.

Clearly, to our twentieth-century eyes, something other than an analysis of operations is driving the layout of this manufacturing complex. Take, for example, the blacksmiths' building. It makes our kind of sense that the forges be in the center, near the entrance. But why are the storerooms for charcoal and iron at the ends of the building? Our mind's eye envisions a videotape of ironwork being dragged back and forth (right past the workers' rooms!) from storeroom to forge and back again.

But we know that to think that way is to think anachronistically. What drives Ledoux's design is not the process of ironmongery but the idea of it, its "essence" as that can be expressed in architectural order. Clearly the defining moment in ironmongery is when base stuff is transformed into useful tools; the people who do the work, and the base materials themselves, are only contributory to that moment. So Ledoux expresses *that,* placing the great belching forges in the honorific central pavilion, and the workers and storerooms (undifferentiated on the exterior) in the subsidiary wings.

But to discuss only the working parts of Chaux is to ignore the 800-pound gorilla of the complex, the director's building. Its great height, giant columns, and decoration only confirm what its geomet-

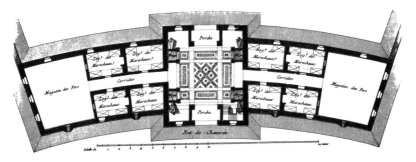

Royal Saltworks at Chaux, plan of blacksmiths' building

rical position makes plain: this is the center of the operation. Several commentators have remarked how this positioning symbolizes *surveillance* (the director's building looks out on radiating lines at the workers' houses; and it and the overseers' houses stare down the length of the salt-making sheds); and you yourself can probably find other readings in the geometrical relationships of the plan.

But the reading which the plan will *not* support is the one modern factories present to us, that of a diagram of the production process. When Ledoux was presented with the problem of designing a salt-works, that is not what he seized upon. To his way of thinking, the proper approach was to imagine the social relationships of the place and then make them visible through architecture. And following Alberti, he believed that geometry would provide him with the tools to map those relationships into space. Even if the need for salt caused Chaux to be built, what Ledoux and his patrons hoped to accomplish there was to provide an instance of the idea of a productive social organization.[10] And for people of the ancien régime, a productive society in the mold of France under the control of the king seemed the proper model.

But look closely at the control point of this little society, the director's building, for with it we can detect a subtle but important shift in thinking about to take place. For all the centrality of the director's building, from no point in it is it possible actually to spy on workers and monitor their activities. This is not the actuality but the idea of surveillance. This is what you do when your intention is to instance surveillance rather than to accomplish it.

But in 1797, the mere idea of surveillance was not enough for Jeremy Bentham: to his way of thinking, only actual accomplished surveillance would do. And so he came up with the idea of the Panopticon, a kind of principle of building organization that could be used wherever it was important to keep an eye on people—in, for example, a workhouse for paupers. Here, all the pie-wedge rooms open off a circular gallery, and by walking the circuit of that gallery, an overseer can look into each of the rooms in turn.

In the contrast between these two forms of surveillance is the break between the building seen as an instantiator of order (Ledoux) and the building seen as an effectuator of results (Bentham).

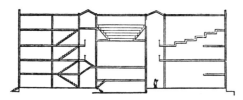

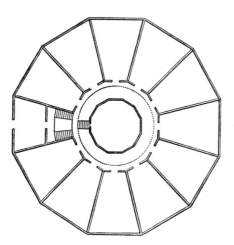

Jeremy Bentham, design for a paupers' workhouse

Bentham is thinking about building in a way wholly different from Ledoux. What masks the difference is the fact that a similar ordered geometry serves their very different ends. So let's look at a building where ordered geometry was not able to bring about the desired results.

freeze-frame:

Royal Victoria Hospital, Belfast, 1903

Reyner Banham made a career of promoting buildings and places snubbed by the standard architectural histories, and he took this particular orphan under his wing in *The Architecture of the Well-Tempered Environment*—which is fitting, for the issue driving its design is ventilation.

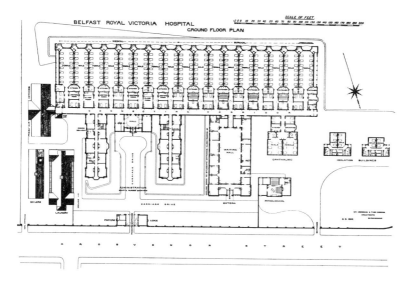

Royal Victoria Hospital, Belfast, plan

It had been presumed for over a century that fresh air was important to health, and so hospital designers had evolved the strategy of stretching patient wards into long, thin wings, the better to catch the breezes. But in Belfast the breezes were likely to be loaded with soot, and so the managers of the Royal Victoria Hospital determined that their patients would get their air through mechanical means, so that it could be cleaned before delivery. To accomplish this, the plan of the patient wards was made almost a diagram of the ventilation process.

Steam-powered fans (housed in the building to the left of the patient block) drew air through filtering curtains of wet rope and then propelled it, heated in winter, down a 500-foot-long duct beneath a connecting corridor (the duct was in fact the whole space beneath the corridor, nine feet wide and tapering in height from twenty feet to six). From the left-hand side of the duct, distributor channels carried the air past operating rooms and kitchens into the side walls of the top-lit wards. The air then rose inside the walls and was delivered into the wards from grilles high up under the ceiling. An answering system of air exhaust drew off stale air from inlets in the baseboards and carried it to ventilating turrets at the ends of the side walls.[11]

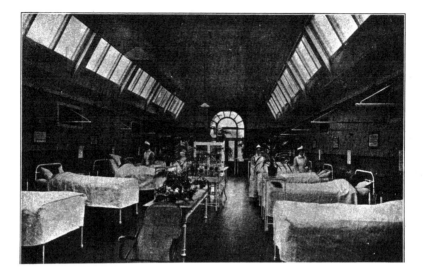

Royal Victoria Hospital, Belfast, typical patient ward

We can see without question that results govern the plan of the patient wards. And it looks like results, and not ideas about order, govern the overall plan as well, with blocks for other services (administration, doctors' offices, eye exams) "clipped onto" the corridor, the whole plan ready (to our eyes if not to those of the time) for expansion to the left to meet new needs.

But look at each of those "clip-on" blocks. Without a clear imperative of results to be accomplished, the architects fall back on architectural order as their governing idea. And so the administration block is wrenched into a French *cour d'honneur*, pairs of its essentially identical offices bumped out to form a cross-axis and Louvre-derived end pavilions.

Clearly such moves are meaningless. In the discourse of order, to accentuate a space is to say that it is more important than spaces left plain. Ledoux said that about the forges in his blacksmith building, and to the mind of his time, that design statement spoke meaningfully about results as well. In the post-Bentham world we gauge results differently. Here in the administration block, "results thinking" wants a number of equal and interchangeable spaces. "Design thinking" believes that only a graduated hierarchy of spaces is appropriate for an entrance. And so the two discourses talk past each other. In the end, results thinking gets its equal spaces, but they're compromised; and design thinking gets its hierarchy, but it is meaningless.

Even where results thinking gets its way, as it does in the patient-ward block, there is nonetheless the problem of how to make it look—an issue about which results thinking has very little to say. To look at the elevations of the ward block is to see architects thoroughly at sea about what to do ("Do we highlight the vent turrets or the end windows of the wards? In any case, we better make the end turrets bigger so as to turn the corners convincingly."). Banham character-izes their answer to the dilemma as like the "'Welfare' architecture fathered by the London School Board some forty years before."[12]

The conflict between results and design is at base a conflict be-tween rationalization and convention, a conflict introduced into our world when Enlightenment minds like Bentham's showed us a new way of thinking. Ever after, we are left with the problem: when you have to invent something (like a new hospital), how do you come to a decision that you have invented "correctly"? Do you accede to what

Royal Victoria Hospital, Belfast, view of ward block

rational analysis reveals to you, or do you try to conform your invention to what has conventionally been done?

But there was another gift of the Enlightenment, the idea of the "invisible hand" of the marketplace. Akin to rationalization, it asks us to make that decision about what to do by acceding to what the marketplace reveals to us. In our next stopping point, architects feel their design values under attack from both rationalization and the market.

freeze-frame:

Architecture: A Profession or an Art?, 1892

In 1891 a bill was introduced in Parliament mandating that architects be licensed and that licensure be granted by examination. The bill failed, but several prominent British architects were moved to speak against the idea, and their thoughts were collected in a book. Their objections are many, and reading them, one can't escape the mental image of mustachioed clubmen in wing chairs harrumphing from behind their copies of *The Times*. But their words do give voice to architecture's conception of itself in the moment just before modernism.

Some objected to the very idea of testing. Certain that an examination could test only quantifiable matters, they feared that "the quantifiable" would come to be seen as the essence of architecture, a gross misconception in their eyes.[13] Others saw the quantification threat in larger terms, as the rise of a rationalizing turn of mind inimical to both the creation and appreciation of architecture.

One rationalizing trend was the increasing importance placed on *drains* (which we would call plumbing, and by extension, mechanical services). One of the arguments being advanced for licensure was the need "to lay our drains so as not to poison us."[14] A surprising number of the writers inveighed on this subject, and we can easily see why. Piping has its own logic of sizes and slopes, but this logic seldom accords with the conventions of architectural order. Under some Murphy's Law of Plumbing, a pipe seems always to need to run across a wall opening or beneath a ceiling. The problem is that the logic of piping is implacable (it has both rational science and public

health behind it), whereas the logic of architecture has only convention to back it up. Our clubmen were encountering that conflict in
their practices and, having neither theory nor convention to help
them solve the problem, they were feeling beset by it.

And they were feeling beset as well by rationally engineered structure. From ancient times onward, architecture was masonry, and the
weight and thickness that masonry requires for structural soundness
had come to define how architecture should look and feel. But now
comes the problem of steel:

Purely scientific construction—that is, the application of mathematics to
calculate and use the minimum of material—is not true architectural construction, and the nearer it approaches to the irreducible minimum, the
farther it is from architecture."[15]

Ernest Newton refers disdainfully to "certain members of the 'profession'" who would see the term "construction" as referring solely
to iron columns and beams. In this he almost certainly refers to
Viollet-le-Duc, whom you will meet later in this chapter. But Newton
frames the problem precisely when he states, apropos of "surveyors"
(read "engineers"):

A public more or less ignorant of architecture has gradually come to demand of an architect qualifications entirely foreign to his calling, and these
demands have been conceded one by one, until by the process of evolution
the foreign elements have become the natural ones, and a new species is
formed—the "architect and surveyor."

In his eyes, architecture was under attack from a way of thinking not
just inimical to architectural values but gaining dominance in the
public mind, the architect now having "to impress his ideas on the
minds of a more mechanical race of interpreters."[16]

And more bad news. Rationalization was convincing the public not
just with its mechanical and engineering feats but with its apparent
ability to reduce the price of things. In construction, rational analysis
was revealing techniques and materials that were much cheaper than
those conventionally used. People engaged in such cost cutting were
called then (as they still are) "jerry-builders," and for all the disdain
the term implies, our Victorian architects had a grudging appreciation for their rationalizing skill:

In his own bad way, the jerry-builder is a master of construction, and if he did not know how to build well he would never be able to build so badly.[17]

But the objection to the jerry-builder was not really that he built so badly (although some did); it was rather that he was convincing people that what he did, at cut-rate prices, was just as good as the high-priced spread that architects were offering.

In no other way could the citizen house himself in a "villa" for a rent which would only provide a superior cottage if built substantially.[18]

For such a citizen the quality that made a villa a villa was its appearance. Of little value to him were intrinsic qualities: Was it truly made of what it appeared to be made of? Was it constructed in the best possible manner? Appearance being all, he would naturally choose the house that achieved the look he wanted at the lowest cost to him, regardless of how that look had been achieved.

So our architects had heard the debate on the registration bill and had concluded that the bill was only the visible sign of a more pervasive problem. For them architecture could be created and appreciated only by a mind that valued conventions of order and intrinsic qualities. Yet they faced a public increasingly ruled by the turn of mind that judges solely on the basis of price, and that values the rationalized solution above all.

Our architects proposed solutions to the dilemma, from political action to an advocacy of craft to solidarity with artisans, but none was convincing. What I hope is convincing, however, is the solution suggested, curiously enough, by an artifact that was both rationalized and cheap: the Model T Ford.

freeze-frame:

Henry Ford's *My Life and Work*, 1922

It's hard to imagine, today, the hold that Henry Ford once had on the American imagination: in each year of the 1920s, an average of 145 stories on Ford in the *New York Times;*[19] five times the press citations of Charlie Chaplin or Mary Pickford.[20] In 1923 just under half of all cars produced on earth were Fords.[21] In the late 1920s, Ford was the largest manufacturer of commercial airplanes,[22] and in 1918 the largest *movie* distributor on earth.[23] Little wonder then that his ghost-written autobiography was a best-seller for months in the United States and Europe (in Germany, topping major fiction works),[24] and was translated into twelve languages.[25] And the car that started it all was the legendary Model T.

For Ford the Model T was not so much a car as a credo. In 1909 he announced:

I will build a car for the great multitude. It will be large enough for the family but small enough for the individual to run and care for. It will be constructed of the best materials, by the best men to be hired, after the simplest designs that modern engineering can devise. But it will be so low in price that no man making a good salary will be unable to own one— and enjoy with his family the blessing of hours of pleasure in God's great open spaces.[26]

Cheap and rationalized. Cheap it was, with the price continually reduced as production efficiency increased. The price drops, though, reflected only Ford the marketer and social theorist. Rationalization engaged Ford's engineering soul. Rationalization was a process that never ended, and it would never end on his Model T.

We cannot conceive how to serve the consumer unless we make for him something that, as far as we can provide, will last forever. We want the man who buys one of our products never to have to buy another. We never make an improvement that renders any previous model obsolete. The parts of a specific model . . . are interchangeable with similar parts on all cars that we have turned out. You can take a car of ten years ago and, buying today's parts, make it with very little expense into a car of today.[27]

When you bought a Model T you were not just buying a product, you were buying into the process that was going to make a better world. Little wonder then that Americans took the Model T to their hearts, formed clubs, gave it names like "Tin Lizzie."[28]

And little wonder that architects like Le Corbusier could see, in the continuing rationalization of cars, an analog to the historical development of architecture—and a conception of its possible future. One of the many possible ways to interpret the impact of Le Corbusier, and modernist ideas generally, is to say that they taught architecture to see rationalization as an ally. Or perhaps it's truer to say that through modernism, architecture was reconceived so as to include a version of rationalization within itself.

In either case it's worth noting that today, unlike our Victorian clubmen, we architects can feel enthusiasm over the project of applying "mathematics to calculate and use only the minimum of material." From the example of the modernists and especially Louis Kahn we have learned to appreciate the rationalized management of mechanical services so that we, like Reyner Banham, look at the patient wards of the Royal Victoria Hospital and see in their planning a foretelling of what we do and how we think today.

But if the rationalization of engineering has been incorporated into architectural thinking, what of that other aspect of the Model T, its cheapness? What about the rationalizing done by the marketplace?

To understand what the Model T teaches us about the market, we have to turn the calendar back to Henry Ford's childhood. Ford was a man of agrarian and small-town nineteenth-century America. His memories were filled with images of farmers and artisans just barely getting by. And because of those memories, industrialization was to him something of a miracle. To Ford it was

self-evident that the majority of people are incapable of producing with their own hands a sufficient quantity of goods which can be exchanged for what they need to live. It is only because planning, management, and tool-building are in place that they are able to produce enough value that they can live well.[29]

Ford saw manufacturing as the magic means by which people who could only manage subsistence by their individual efforts could, by banding together under industrial management, achieve sufficiency. It was to those people moving from subsistence to sufficiency that he directed his Model T. For those people, the Model T—stripped-down to the basics ("any colour . . . so long as it is black"[30]), incrementally improvable but only with "rational" improvements—matched their aspirations exactly.

But what happens when sufficiency is achieved? Rationalization had shown itself capable of lifting people from subsistence to sufficiency, but could it carry them farther? The answer, Ford soon found, was no.

Hear this 1926 letter to Ford from a B. F. O'Brien of Moline, Illinois:

Right outside my window stands a Ford, a Star and an Essex, and across the street a Chevrolet and a Pontiac. The owner of each of these traded in a Ford. In fact, they never owned anything else but a Ford until this year, and the fellow who still has the Ford is about to buy an Essex.

When O'Brien asked his neighbors why, they all said that they had found the Model T economical and relatively trouble-free, but now they were "bored. They wanted something different. A change."[31]

They had moved into the world of sufficiency. Part of this was Ford's own doing. He had championed the principle of paying workers wages high enough to buy the products they made, his "Five Dollar Day" sparking in 1915 the revolution that would lift industrial workers into the middle class.[32] By the mid-1920s, enough people saw themselves in that way that Model T sales began to decline; people who saw themselves as beyond subsistence no longer identified with Ford's astringent vision of prudent, rational improvement. When you don't have enough, "enough" will satisfy you, but once you've got enough, you have the luxury of wondering about the possibility of something "different."

Alfred P. Sloan, president of the then-upstart General Motors, caught the new spirit of the times when he introduced yearly model changes, saying that one function of the new car models was to create "a certain amount of dissatisfaction" with the old ones.[33]

Ford finally responded, late in 1927, with the new Model A. To meet the challenge of GM's new models, he was forced to abandon the incremental upgrade principle (all the new changes simply couldn't be reconciled back onto an eighteen-year-old chassis); he was forced to abandon the T's planetary-gear transmission (elegant in its rationality but quirky under real driving conditions); he was forced into "irrational" styling, and even colors.[34]

So how, you are entitled to ask, does all this help us think more clearly about the design of buildings? Remember what got us onto the subject of cars in the first place, the question that faces anyone who creates things (cars or buildings): When you have to judge what you have invented, what voice do you listen to? What conventional order says? Or what rational analysis reveals? Or what the marketplace decides?

Our Victorian clubmen could hear only one voice, that of convention, which laid out for them the recognized list of ordering schemes and construction methods for buildings. Modernism then recast architecture's conception of order. We now see the revelations of rational analysis being fully as ordered as those handed down to us by convention. When the voice of convention says of our design, "That's not ordered," we heed that judgment and rethink. When analysis says, "That's not rational," we heed that as well because, to our way of thinking, it is also saying, "That's not ordered." The two conceptions of order are not identical, of course, but we believe them to be reconcilable to the point where we can speak of them in a single language. Architects today don't need a separate discourse to talk about rationalization. We can talk about it and conventional order in a single design language.

But then comes the market, whose voice must be heeded because unless the marketplace's judgments of our inventions are in the affirmative, they will not get built. How does the market make its decisions? The answer is simple: upon the single criterion that can be phrased variously as, "Does it work? Does it sell? Does it return a profit?"

The market's criteria of judgment are all external: how does the world respond to what we do? Unlike rationalization or conventional order, it has no criteria internal to itself that judge an action "good" or "bad." The market is in that sense free of internal values.

And that is its great usefulness. It can try out propositions that other fields of endeavor would constrain themselves from trying, due to the judgments made by their internal value structures ("We can't do that: it's not rational; it's not ordered."). The market expands for us the realm of the possible. Its nature is to push the envelope, blind to the consequences. Society's job in such a system is to design the envelope, to set the limits of where the market can go, expecting that the market will push right up against them. For in showing us what's possible within those boundaries, the market will give us the data we as a society need to be able to decide whether to shrink or enlarge or change them.

Again, the market is without internal values. So when Model T's were offered up for judgment and the market said "yes," that was no sign that the market and rationalization operated under similar principles (that was Ford's misperception, and Le Corbusier's). It was merely that, for the moment, what analysis judged "rational" the market judged "a hot item"—an entirely different standard of judgment. And so when qualities other than rationalization made a car a hot item, the market went in that direction. It had used rationalization because it had sold. Now that something else sold, it would use that instead.

Similarly for our architect of the commercial frontage in a previous chapter. In the design phase, "rationalized order" looked, to the market-oriented client, like it would sell, and so he had given his architect the go-ahead. From that positive judgment the architect had allowed himself to imagine that design order and the marketplace operated on similar principles. Not so. The minute The Gap called up, the market went elsewhere. To meet its criterion of "finding what works," it could do nothing else.

Can we characterize this internal imperative? I would propose *substitution* to describe what drives the market. It wants to convince people to choose a new item over the one they now have. To invent those new offerings, the market might call on rationalization, or it might call on creation pure and simple. It might find rationalization useful in a world characterized by subsistence, when no one has the product yet, or has only a very primitive version of it (as was the case for modernist architects with the homeless of World War I needing mass-produced housing, and for Ford with farmers driving horse-and-buggy). Or, for a world of sufficiency, it might find its ends served better by creation for novelty's sake.

But in neither case is the market adopting the philosophical attitude behind the invention process. It is no more committed to novelty than it is to rationality. It has no philosophy, other than to listen to what the marketplace says. If the marketplace says, "I want to substitute your product for the one I now have," then that product will have been adjudged proper and correct, regardless of the process by which it was invented.

So if the market calls upon the architect to produce a building that rationalizes, that advances the state of the art, it is not because the market wants the state of the art advanced. It is because state-of-the-art will, at this particular moment, sell: it will convince someone to substitute this new office or hospital or school for the one they're now occupying.

Similarly, if the market asks from the architect a building of absolute novelty—or a building that hews absolutely to received conventions of order—no endorsement should be read from this charge, no coincidence of interests.

So to distinguish this marketplace kind of "results" thinking from the rationalizing turn of mind, let's give the name *Market discourse* to this way of seeing the building. And to establish in our minds the distinctions between the three discourses, let's adopt a common framework for characterizing all three, so that differences among them will stand out and stick in our minds.

When in a discourse you talk about a building *as* something, the reason you are doing that kind of talking is that you hope to bring into existence *that kind of building*. A discourse then is actually a mode of working, the work as it develops being discussed and evaluated by thought and speech. So to characterize a discourse, we need to characterize first the kind of building that the discourse wants, and then the nature of the work that brings it about.

So, I offer four questions that we can ask of all three discourses:

• Why do we engage in this discourse? What kind of building are we trying to get?
• What is the nature of the work we do in this discourse?
• What are we trying to accomplish with our work?
• How do we judge when our work is successful?

In the Market discourse, we are trying to get a building that will bring about results in the marketplace. The work we do in the discourse is invention, and out of that work we are trying to formulate proposals to the marketplace. We will know we are successful when our proposal achieves substitution.

Seems a mighty little conclusion for a mighty lot of argumentation. But I wanted you to have a shorthand version that you can hold in your head as you hear even more argumentation in the next section, this time on the discourse about values.

2b From Values to Community

In the last section we arrived at the proposition that, when speaking of the building in the Market way, the goal that directs how you think and speak is marketplace substitution. What then might be the analogous principle that governs speaking of the building as an embodier of values? Let's begin by returning to Alberti's *Art of Building,* where he is describing the design of a house for a man of means.

freeze-frame:

Alberti's *De re aedificatoria,* 1486

Clearly, some of the house is occupied by members of the family, and the rest is given over to storing items for use. The family consists of the husband, wife, children, and grandparents, and their live-in domestics, including the clerks, attendants, and servants. Any guest is to be included in the family. The items to be stored comprise essentials, such as food, and conveniences, such as clothing, weapons, books, and perhaps even a horse. The most important part is that which we shall call the "bosom" of the house, although you might refer to it as the "court" or "atrium"; next in importance comes the dining room, followed by private bedrooms, and finally living rooms. Then come the remainder, according to their use. The "bosom" is therefore the main part of the house, acting like a public forum, toward which all the lesser members converge.[1]

Alberti goes on from this to describe each of the rooms of the house, in terms of practicality and from the standpoint of what is appropriate for the station of the person to be accommodated; for example:

The young men over seventeen should be accommodated opposite the guests, or at least not far from them, to encourage them to form an acquaintance. Off the guest rooms should be a repository, where the guest might hide his more personal belongings, and retrieve them as he wishes. Off the room for the young men should be the armory.[2]

Alberti states, with a certainty that strikes us as presumptuous, just what all young bachelors will need and how they should act. We know of course, from the last section, that for Alberti this is not presumption. He is merely stating what constitutes part of *virtù* for an unmarried Florentine man of good family, and by extension, for all the members of the household.

But if *virtù* accounts for Alberti's "presumption" about how individuals will act, what explains his equally assured prescription for the whole house, its organization around a central atrium? To get at Alberti's thinking on this matter, we have to divest ourselves of two ideas central to our present-day mode of thought. The first is the idea of the autonomous individual seeking his or her own private vision of the good life. The second is the idea of the state as something that regulates the arena in which people do that seeking but is apart from the individuals themselves.[3]

In Alberti's world, the good life was not something you defined for yourself, it was defined *for you* by the community in which you lived, and you could achieve it only within that community. The things that constituted the good life were defined in such a way that they could only be conferred by others, or they would have meaning only if seen and known by others, or they could be achieved only by all in common.

Because my good life is bound up with everyone else's, the state is not something that stands apart from all of us, regulating our individual actions. The state *is* us; the community is not just the setting but the very means by which we in company pursue the human good.[4]

This was the principle on which all of Florentine society was organized, in diminishing hierarchy: I derive my identity from my membership in my city, my clan, my household, my family; whatever human goods I can achieve, I can achieve them only through the action of the group to which I belong.[5]

So when Alberti describes the relationship between guests and the household, he does so with the assurance with which we today would describe the legal status of foreign visitors to the United States, for to him they would have been one in the same, the one the proper model for the other. And when he describes the atrium as like a public forum toward which all the lesser parts of the house converge,

Alberti is not offering a mere illustrative simile. He is stating to Florentines what they would immediately accept as fact: the house should be organized in the pursuit of its household good as the city is organized in the pursuit of society's good. Like the city, the house would comprise individual quarters, each outfitted according to its station, each related to other spaces according to its function in the household's common pursuit of its proper good life. In emerging from their quarters and meeting in the atrium, the members of the household would feel a resonant echo of the times when they had, as a body, entered into the civic plaza to meet other households on great public events.

This being the case, how could you even imagine designing a house in any other way? Certainly there is no need for a discussion, separate from talk about design order, concerning which values a house would embody. But in later times the issue will indeed come up, and most pointedly in the design of servants' quarters, with the question of whose values should govern their design. So let's listen to Alberti's description of accommodations deemed proper for servants in the Florentine scheme of things. Note another revealing instance of that Foucault *strangeness* (or perhaps not) in what Alberti includes under the rubric of servants' accommodations.

The butlers, domestics, and servants should be segregated from the gentry, and allocated accommodation decorated and furnished in keeping with their positions. The maids and valets should be stationed close enough to their areas of responsibility to enable them to hear commands immediately and be at hand to carry them out. The butler should be stationed at the entrances to the wine cellar and food stores. The stable boys should sleep in front of the stables. The stud horses should be kept apart from the pack horses, in a place where they will not offend anyone inside the house with their smell, or harm one another fighting, and where there is no risk of fire.[6]

freeze-frame:

Entretiens sur l'architecture, 1858–1872

It's hard to overemphasize the importance, to modern architectural thought, of Eugène Emmanuel Viollet-le-Duc's *Discourses on Architecture*. This series of sixteen periodically issued lectures convinced us of the idea of deriving the shape of architecture from a close study of the materials of which it is made. But in the course of developing his arguments, Viollet often steps to one side to offer tangential thoughts (much in the manner of Alberti) that reveal much about the man and his times.[7]

One of these tangents concerns domestic life in the medieval period (as chief restorer of Gothic monuments in France, he had made a close study of the society of those times). He makes the point that in aristocratic societies, servants and masters could freely intermingle in the same spaces in the house, since by custom and law neither "would ever forget the social distance that separated them."[8]

Viollet's description, which probably conjured up in his mind a monochrome woodcut, evokes in us the technicolor image of a vast smoky hall presided over by the gentry at their long groaning board, the lord of the manor ripping great, greasy bites out of a joint of beef, servants and jesters and musicians swirling around in what looks to us like perfect chaos. How, the scene makes us ask, could anyone think, much less engage in courtly conversation, with such distractions? Of course, as Viollet reminds us, to the gentry the servants' ministrations would have been no distraction at all. In all likelihood their presence intruded on the gentry's consciousness no more than stereo equipment does on ours.

But in mid-nineteenth-century France, Viollet observed, the presence of servants was very much felt by the families who employed them. What had changed? In the intervening years the idea of democracy had been introduced. That idea contended in people's minds with the surviving distinctions of rank, called those distinctions into question, and thus made master and servant uneasy in each other's presence. Universally accepted conventions of behavior and hierarchy once had erected a social distance between groups. Now democracy collapsed that distance. The solution to the problem was to reerect the distance, but now physically, with walls.[9] And so domestic architecture developed elaborate strategies for separating servants from masters: separately entered servants' quarters, back stairs and passageways, the ideal being that servants could pop out from their spaces when needed but would otherwise be invisible.

We will be looking in a moment at the stages by which this "ideal" was accomplished, but we can't leave Viollet without first hearing the paradox he uncovers in this development.

Domestic architecture in an aristocratic state may affect a breadth and simplicity which would be intolerable in a democratic condition.[10]

The buildings of autocratic times look and feel broad, open—*democratic*—while those of democratic times seem pinched, full of hierarchies and "secret places."[11]

Or, to put it more broadly, when the beliefs of a society and its social structures are in harmony, architecture can be designed along ideal lines. (A discourse on design order is nearly sufficient as a way of talking about a building.) But when social structures give the lie to what a society says it believes, then architecture gets used as a tool in the management of the conflict. (A second discourse, in conflict with that about order, comes increasingly into play.)

Viollet's observation implies a hard truth: until true democracy is achieved, we will never be able to build an architecture that looks and feels democratic; and if we attempt to build such architecture now, it will be propaganda, a false statement that belief and actuality have been brought into concord.

Until that time, we are left with what might be called Viollet's rule: the shakier the conventions, the greater the need for precision in the design of the plan, and for thought about the values to guide that precision. Watch now as the democratic idea forces architecture into greater and greater precision.

freeze-frame:

The English country house, 1200–1900

In a series of books social historian Mark Girouard has tracked the relationship between the lives people led and the houses and towns they lived in. *Life in the English Country House* shows us the houses that the British upper classes built for themselves from the medieval period up to the "Indian summer" between the world wars. Girouard gives us a schema that periodizes the houses into coherent eras, but we want to take those houses and ask a slightly different question of them.

What values were the elite embodying in the parts of the houses they built for themselves, and what values were embodied in the quarters they provided for their servants? In the answers to that question we will see demonstrated Viollet's thesis that as values come under challenge, spaces become more particularized, for both master and servant.

Girouard reminds us that in medieval times, society was a galaxy of clans, each headed by a hereditary lord, and each comprising a complete hierarchy of roles, from servants to artisans through a dependent gentry on up to the lord's own family at the top. And all lived (or spent the most consequential parts of their days) in the manor house. It was a society akin to Alberti's, but without the overarching identity and governance of a city-state. And as in Alberti's Florence, the hierarchy of the household was a rock-solid explanation, accepted by all, of how life is and how it should be conducted.

The great hall embodied this vision of life. When the lord presided at his table, with the gentry arrayed below him by rank with all manner of folk milling about, the scene looked like a patriarch having a great meal with his extended family—which was precisely how the lord and his subjects saw themselves.[12] Like the Florentine piazza or palazzo atrium, the hall was the vehicle by which the hierarchy made itself visible to itself, on organized state occasions and in what we today would call "hanging out" (with servants to do most of the work, the gentry had hours of time to kill).

But equally emblematic of the value structure is what happened when the hubbub in the hall died down and it came time to go to bed. As in Alberti's palazzo, servants like stablehands, whose work was for the whole household, slept next to their work. But personal servants slept near their masters, on fold-away pallets, in the lord's chamber and in the apartments assigned to family members and live-in gentry. They were there to fetch a glass of water, supply an extra blanket, carry away the bed pan, and ease a robe onto the master's shoulders when he awoke.

It's hard for us today to imagine how the medieval elite conceptualized their servants. Was it something like the way we today think of

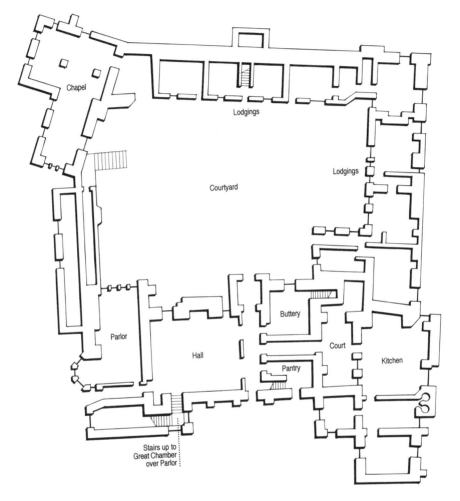

Haddon Hall, twelfth to fifteenth centuries, plan

equipment? Certainly they functioned as equipment—faucet, electric blanket, toilet, closet. Or, given the "extended family" nature of the household, did the elite have for their servants that vague "a part of us" feeling we today might have for small children distantly related to us? Or, given their faithfulness and obedience, did servants occupy in their masters' minds the place that pets now fill in ours—their nearby presence at night a reassuring comfort? Perhaps their thoughts contained aspects of all three.

Whatever the masters may have thought, we know the stark impossibility of our ever thinking *that*. But we can say with certainty that in their masters' minds, servants were incapable of independent volition. And to imagine them having their own values, different from those that governed the household—we can feel fairly sure that neither the masters nor their servants could think that.

As the Jacobean period approached, society did come gradually to gain an overarching sense of governance and identity, in the person of the king. The households lost their sense of being "all there is of society," and (as a consequence?) that all-encompassing feeling of family diminished. The constant presence of the entire household, which once had felt comforting, now began to feel smothering. And so the lord (the one person who could freely act upon his feelings) began, in stages, to retreat from his position of *paterfamilias* immersed in the midst of his adoring household.

The first stage was for the lord's family to have most of their meals in a "great chamber" off the hall, with the upper gentry standing in for the master at the high table, positioned, significantly, at the end of the hall nearest the great chamber.[13] In the next development, it became the practice for the gentry to eat with the lord in his chamber (leaving the hall the province of the lower orders and the hangers-on), and so the lord now needed a chamber beyond the great chamber into which he could withdraw for privacy and for sleeping.[14] And when, still later, lords began to take meals in that second chamber, yet another, deeper, chamber was required for privacy and sleep.[15]

What this centuries-long development conjures to our cinema-trained minds is, of course, a Monty Python image of the lord being backed into smaller and smaller rooms by a mob of gesticulating petitioners and lackeys. But there's a kernel of insight in the comic image. As his rock-solid social structure comes to seem less "ordained," as its distinctions of rank lose some of their force, the lord erects walls to gain distance, to assert the distinctions that convention seems less and less able to make stick.

In spite of this, as the lord retreats through his chambers in our imaginary film, his servant accompanies him, sleeping in the inner-

From Values to Community

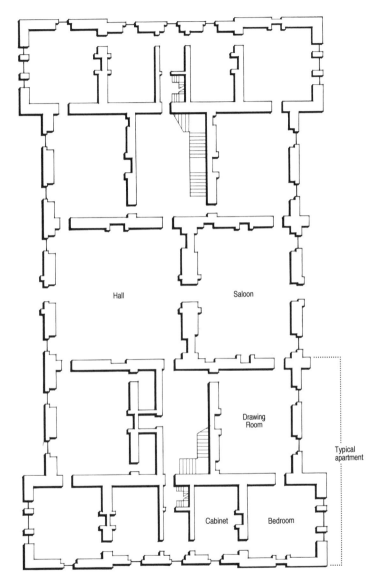

Houghton Hall, 1720s, plan

most room where the lord sleeps. At the end of the sequence though, at the beginning of the 1600s, the servant is installed in a small cubicle just off the bedchamber, invisible but instantly available. Does this imply that the lord thinks the servant "deserves a room of his own"? Hardly. The cubicle that contains the servant's pallet often also contains the lord's close-stool, his portable toilet.[16] The servant is still equipment. In the mind of the lord he has value, but not values.

Or to see the matter differently: The walls of the suite of chambers are there to enforce the differentiation of people by groups (only the highest gentry get into the private dining room, the next-highest gentry get no farther than the outer chamber, and so on down the ranks). Servants aren't a part of this schema. Some of them, like the fire tenders, bustle through the rooms indiscriminately; others move in the system as an attachment to their masters. Servants aren't yet conceived of as *a group* and so aren't a fit object for the new walling-off strategy of distinction maintenance.

But by the eighteenth century, everything had changed. The system of fealty to a lord in return for protection and identity had given way, replaced by a monarch and a standing army. The unlanded gentry now had other means of advancement—in government service,[17] or in the cities. And as the gentry came to see their interests as similar to those of the merchants and professions,[18] all the former positions in the old manor hierarchy sorted themselves into a new social order, at the bottom of which were the small land holders, land tenants, and servants,[19] now clearly defined as *a group* by their shared attribute of having been the leftovers from the great postmanor shakeout process.

The great landowners (no longer composed just of hereditary lords) now found themselves, post-shakeout, in a new situation. No longer competing with each other, either for territory or for the favor of the king, they now saw each other not as rivals but as allies with common interests, members of the same class. Plus, the societal obligations of the old system were gone, but the land (and therefore the wealth) was still intact. And so the landowning classes embarked on a round of entertaining that lasted for two centuries, and they fashioned their houses accordingly.

The first shape these houses took was that of a great circuit of rooms around which guests would proceed in the course of a long party.[20] Gone was the hierarchy-enforcing telescope of chambers. No need for that now: the only people at these parties would be "people like us," people who were not just of our rank but who shared our values and our conventions of behavior.

So since there were now no distinctions to be enforced, the architecture was relieved of that responsibility and could become "broad and open." And since everyone would know how to act, the spaces could be arrayed in a pleasing, "ideal" composition: people would know how to navigate the arrangement even though it gave them few cues.[21]

How, though, would servants be conceptualized in such a world? Their presence while working the party would not beset the guests with thoughts about inequity: these guests would have had no more doubt about the position of servants in this new hierarchy of classes than the lords and gentry had about their positions in the old hierarchy of the manor. But this new elite didn't think of their servants as a part of their person in the way the lords did. Servants were now *a group*, something unto themselves and apart from us. (They must now be sought out, from their own people, and *employed*.) And being a group, and not a part of us, they belonged together, in their own space apart from ours. But where?

The solution that satisfied—putting the servants' quarters on the ground floor (with the overflow tucked up under the roof)—served several practical purposes but also reveals something of the thought of the time. Putting the servants' spaces there meant that the circuit of rooms would be lifted up, endowed with more importance. Plus, the prime rooms could then display their ideal symmetries unencumbered. And goods and tradesmen could be gotten in and out of the ground floor easily and discreetly.

But using the servants' spaces as the base of the house also accorded with the categorical thinking that we saw Ledoux using in the design of the saltworks at Chaux. Ranking "service" as subsidiary to "living" diagrammed the proper relationship between the two components of the whole, just as the blacksmith's building diagrammed the proper relationship of its components.

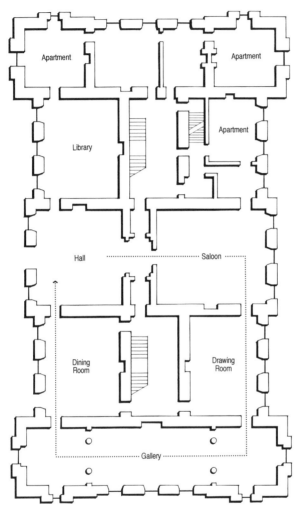

Hagley Hall, 1750s, plan

How then to arrange the spaces within that "service" component? The answer that satisfied was: along much the same categorical lines that Ledoux used when laying out his blacksmiths' rooms and their associated charcoal and iron storage. At Chaux, the wings had been given that size which would comport correctly with the center block (the discourse about order speaking almost unchallenged). Thus sized, the space of the wings was distributed into the categories of living quarters and storage space.

The size and shape of the space for "service" in the great houses was likewise determined pretty much by thinking in terms of order: it was whatever space lay beneath the circuit of rooms ideally proportioned and arranged. The service floor was interpenetrated by whatever structure the rooms above required, and it was lit by whatever openings would align with those that design order had dictated for the rooms above. Once all that was determined, the space could be distributed into categories of service—the kitchen with its related pantries and sculleries, fuel storage and food storage, etc.[22]

So, with distinction making now handled by a settled structure of values and conventions, the walls of the elite's entertaining rooms were relieved of their burden of embodying values and could now embody order instead. When you spoke about the design of a house, the discourse about design order could provide you with just about all you might want to say. And because design thinking had set the placement and sizing of the service areas, it was perfectly reasonable to let the design's categorical thinking determine their layout as well.

By around 1800, though, we are approaching Viollet-le-Duc's world, with its democracy-engendered uneasiness about the equity of the class system and its heightened awareness of servants as people like one's self.[23] Several factors coalesced that first highlighted the problem and then provided its solution.

The first factor was a turn away from the rigidly conventionalized entertaining of the previous era, toward a style more natural and spontaneous. The English house party now came into being, and the country weekend, the essence of both being that between breakfast and dinner, guests were left pretty much on their own to do what they wished.[24] But if convention wasn't dictating what every guest would be doing and when and where, then how would servants know when they were wanted? The answer came in the late eighteenth century with the invention of the bell-pull.[25] Now the guests could call for a servant no matter where their spontaneous amusements might have led them.

But with this turn toward the natural came a desire to have the main rooms of the house on the ground floor, so that views and guests and sometimes the party itself could flow out over the grounds. Where then to put the service spaces? If you were to stick them off in a wing, the symmetry of the house would be compromised. Fortunately, the desire for nature also led to an appreciation of asymmetry, to which a servants' wing could picturesquely contribute.[26]

And so a design solution was set that endured in the country house until its demise in the 1930s: a main house, related informally (or later, more formally) to its grounds, a servants' wing stretching off away from it, the two connected at only a few strategic points, most notably the dining room. In that architectural solution was a social solution: in providing them with their own separate realm, the upper classes were able to feel that they had done right by their servants, and so were able to gain a measure of ease in their presence. The Victorian taste maker Robert Kerr stated the arrangement when he characterized the family as one community and the servants as another, and "each class is entitled to shut its door upon the other and be alone."[27] Until, of course, someone tugs at the bell-pull.

But if there were now these two worlds separated by a baize door, by what sorts of ideas was each designed? To understand the design of the servants' spaces, we have to remember that present at this moment was not just the idea of equity rooted in democracy but also the idea broached by Bentham of the rational analysis of function. We need also to recall that large country houses were essentially small luxury hotels, and their management required the organization and coordination of processes on an almost industrial scale. So when people, armed with the new rationalizing turn of mind, began to think of factories as a flow of materials through a production process, it seemed only natural to design servants' spaces along similar lines.

To examine servants' wings of the nineteenth century is to see production processes made visible. Food preparation provides the most

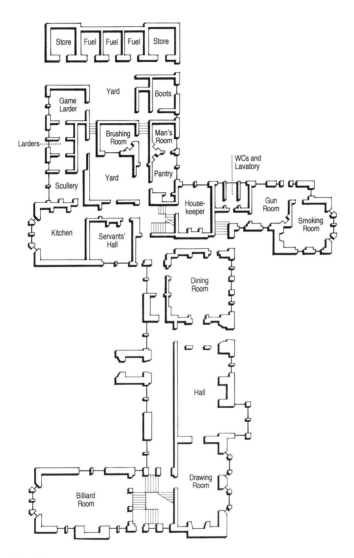

Marshcourt, 1900s, Edwin Lutyens, plan

graphic picture: strings of specialized food-storage spaces converge on a vast kitchen which, in its turn, leads to serving pantries and finally (through that baize door) out to the dining room. Other strings of rooms tell of the processes of removing the cutlery and plates from the table and cleaning, polishing, and storing them for reuse; of taking napery from the table, linens from the beds, and clothes from the dressing rooms and laundering, mending, and pressing them for redeployment; of polishing muddy boots, brushing brambles from overcoats, repairing riding tack, arranging flowers, receiving tradesmen—and all of it laid out, with the precision of a circuitry board, so that the lines of production cross as little as possible.

Clearly this is an environment thought of as a rationalized process, a machine in effect, with the servants functioning as operators and conveyor belts. In discussions about the design of such a place, it's hard to imagine talk about values, or even of order architecturally conceived, having any standing.

But if no discourse about values governed the design of servants' quarters, what of the main house itself? Did the discourse about order still give you all you would want to say, or did the new informality require other ways of speaking?

If our picture of eighteenth-century amusements is one of people chatting and posturing, our vision of an English country weekend (seen, inevitably, through the gauzy lens of *Brideshead Revisited*) is one of people doing things—playing billiards, reading, writing letters, smoking after dinner. These amusements, unlike that mere standing-around of the eighteenth century, required equipment and purpose-built rooms. What is more, some of the activities were sex-segregated. And there were *lots* of potential amusements, more than any one house could accommodate.

So if you and your architect were to set out to design such a house, to be used in these new ways, you would be confronted with issues like: Which amusements appeal to you? Which would appeal to the kind of guests you plan to have? Do you want a library that women will feel comfortable in? What's your preferred setting for reading? For writing letters? How much do you want to invest in billiards equipment? These are *values* questions.

The charge to the architect could no longer be set merely by naming the client's station in society, nor would it be enough to take widely accepted conventions of behavior and interpret them through abstract order. The charge must now be *determined*. And to do that required a discussion about what intentions the client held and how the house would reflect them, a discourse about values.

With this it looks as if we have come at last to a conception of architecture free of that Foucault *strangeness,* architecture discussed and designed as we would do it, almost familiar. But not quite.

If we envision the discussions between a mid-Victorian industrialist and his architect about the house to be erected on his newly acquired estate, it's hard to imagine his wife as an active participant. Even harder to imagine is the involvement of the children or the servants. No, the times would have considered it entirely proper for the husband (or his agent) to speak and decide for the entire household.

freeze-frame:

An American kitchen, 1990

Contrast this with the house-design scenario that is familiar to present-day Americans: the architect, the husband and wife and all the kids gathered around the kitchen table in the old house, everyone gesturing and talking all at once, everyone having a say about the design of the new house, the architect desperately trying to keep up.

I make this comparison not to condemn one approach and praise the other, but to emphasize that both were deemed proper by their respective cultures. And it is not difficult to imagine fully modern cultures of today in which people would follow yet other approaches to determining the charge to the architect.

The general point is this: there is no one correct way to conduct a discourse about values. Who has standing to speak? How much weight is to be accorded to each speaker's words? Are there any values that can trump all others? What conditions will satisfy all concerned that closure has been achieved? Each culture has its own answers for these questions, and they don't necessarily coincide with the answers implicit in the kitchen-table model.

If that is so, then what would be the appropriate way to conduct a "values" discourse in the United States of the present moment? Is it something like our kitchen-table model with its rambunctious equality, its scrappy individualism? I want to argue that it is, but I want to make my argument from a somewhat unusual direction.

In this I recognize that the very idea of a single *anything* being "appropriate for the United States of the present moment" raises all sorts of multicultural hackles. To that I can only reply that the model of discourse I'm about to propose is the property of no one group, is not even closely associated with any one group, but is esteemed by all.

It is frequently remarked that America is not an autochthonous culture but an invented one. It is truer to say that it is a *proposed* culture, described and known but not yet achieved. That is why it is natural for an American to hold a belief incomprehensible to other people—that her culture is not yet fully in place.

We thus partake of a conception we saw in Alberti's world. Every American, from whatever group, feels the distance between "how America is" and "how America could be if it realized its proposition." This being the case, the actions Americans most esteem are those actions that move us from the actual in the direction of that ideal.[28]

The occurrences I am about to describe are of that kind: they show Americans moving toward the attainment of their proposition. They don't "prove" anything about an American discourse of values. They merely illustrate Americans acting out their values. But if it goes too far to claim proof, I think it is fair to say that these actions are *emblematic* of things Americans believe about themselves. To the extent that they are shared beliefs, to that extent they would form the basis for conducting a discourse about values.

freeze-frame:

The Mormon diggings, California, 1848

The name Josiah Royce is not heard much these days, but at the turn of the last century he was one of that circle of illustrious American philosophers that included William James and John Dewey. One of

Royce's lifelong interests was in the ways people form and maintain societies. Paradigmatic for him were the "societies" that miners set up in the Gold Rush California of his boyhood—and none more so than the camps of late summer 1848, which he describes in his *California: A Study of American Character.* One eyewitness, cited by Royce, describes the atmosphere at the camps:

The mines put all men for once upon a level. Clothes, money, manners, family connections, letters of introduction, never before counted for so little . . . Gold was so abundant, and its sources seemed for a time so inexhaustible, that the aggrandizing power of wealth was momentarily annihilated.[29]

Royce's proposition was that, once freed from the distinctions of class and the compulsions of wealth or scarcity, Americans would act in ways that revealed their true "character." While properly suspicious of overly rosy accounts and acknowledging the fragility of the situation, Royce compiles this picture from first-hand accounts:

When they met on any spot to mine, they were accustomed . . . to organize very quickly their own rude and yet temporarily effective government. An alcalde or council, or, in the simplest cases, merely the called meeting of miners decided disputes; and the whole power of the camp was ready to support such decisions . . . In brief, the new mining camp was a little republic, practically independent for a time of the regular State officers, often very unwilling to submit to outside interference even with its criminal justice, and well able to keep its own simple order temporarily intact . . . We read, on good authority, of gold left in plain sight, unguarded and unmolested, for days together; of grave disputes, involving vast wealth, decided by calm arbitration.[30]

But were these merely habits of governance that the miners had carried with them to the camps? More telling for Royce were the arrangements that miners had to invent to cover new circumstances, about which their habits could give no guidance.

One of these new conditions was the operation of the cradle, a kind of portable sluice used for separating gold from sand. In the mechanism water washed gold-bearing earth through a series of seives, leaving, at the end of the sluice, gold dust mixed with a fine sand; when the sand had dried it could be blown away, revealing the heavier gold.

Operating the cradle required four men—one to dig the earth, one to carry it to the cradle and dump it in, a third to rock the cradle side-to-side, and a fourth to pour in the water. To ease fatigue and boredom, the jobs were rotated. But what if the man rocking the sluice saw a glint of gold in the sand: did it belong to him personally or to the team as a whole? What about the man digging the slope, or the man carrying the earth to the cradle: what if either of them saw a nugget?

As reported by Dr. Tyrwhitt Brooks, a British physician recently arrived from Oregon:

> The miners of the Mormon diggings were all conscious, even at this time, of a controlling customary law, quickly formed, as it seemed to them, but at all events derived from no one discoverable present source. Thus it was generally understood that a lump of gold more than half an ounce in weight, if picked up from the freshly dug earth by a member of a party mining in partnership, "before the earth was thrown into the cradle," belonged to the finder personally, and not to the party.[31]

These Edenic conditions fell apart, as we might expect, in the face of accumulating wealth, scarcity at the diggings, intrusive government bureaucracy, and even "civilization" itself when it made possible those trappings by which social hierarchies are promulgated—all of which only underscores Royce's point about essential American values being most clearly visible in those moments when "real world" forces are not in place, when the operations of "what is" is suspended, allowing "what should be" to happen. I will shortly let Royce tell you the conclusions he drew from the mining camps, but before I do, let's look quickly at another instance like that of the cradle team where, because power and wealth were irrelevant, Americans were able to act upon their values in the invention of new customs.

freeze-frame:

The automatic teller machine, 1980–present

I don't know how ATMs first came to your town, but in Richmond, Virginia, they just appeared one day. Our first one showed up in the middle of the bank lobby, on a dais with a velvet rope, like Santa

Claus in a department store, with an attendant like the Fairy Princess to ease you through the new trauma of seeing your money sucked from your hand into a grinding slot. Later the machine migrated to a nearby wall, where it seemed to multiply itself almost monthly. Eventually it left the bank altogether, to pop up around town in all sorts of unexpected places.

What is remarkable though is that from the first moment that we were on our own with ATMs, quickly and with no prompting from the authorities, we Americans invented conventions for using them. You know the customs: wherever you live in the United States, you've probably enacted them yourself.

If there is one machine, you get in line (but not strictly by order of arrival: if you're making a deposit, you get your envelope ready and then join the line; ever notice the scowls when somebody fills out his slip at the machine?). When you advance to the head of the line, you stand no closer than five feet back from the person at the machine, pointedly *not* looking as she keys in numbers (and if your eyes do happen inadvertently to fall upon the screen, you never betray that fact; certainly no eye-rolling comments like "A *ten-dollar* withdrawal?"). If there is more than one machine, you form a *single* line and step up as the next machine becomes free.

To me it's clear that these conventions of behavior stem from a shared esteem for privacy and equality, and a finely honed sense of fairness: it would be unfair (in the sense of "unfair advantage") for you to get in line sooner by not filling out your slip; it would be unfair (in the sense of "undeserved bad consequences") to watch other lines move forward while yours is stuck behind the person doing his whole month's banking.

I realize that this feels like straining after a gnat, making a great to-do over something that is utterly commonplace. But being embedded in a culture is precisely what makes a practice seem ordinary to those of us in the culture: its very *but of course*-ness renders it invisible to us. To really see the practice, we need something that throws it into high relief. First, to feel the force of the values being enacted in the practice, we might try imagining how it could have been otherwise and thus see how those alternative values would offend us. And second, to feel a cultural practice's importance to us, we might imagine the practice under challenge. Let's try two thought experiments to do those two things.

freeze-frame:

The ATM and the Virginia gentleman

The plantation world of eighteenth-century Virginia is the closest America approached to the society of great land owners in contemporaneous England. Rhys Isaac in *The Transformation of Virginia* describes a world of deference and obligation very much like the one we saw in Girouard's country houses, but with peculiar Virginian twists. Through their journals, common folk of the time tell of their awe in the presence of the "splendor" of a gentleman on horseback. But we also hear, in those same journals, accounts of the gentry's reciprocal obligations of "liberality," how they felt obliged to stage public events like horseraces, and to provide spirituous "treats" to all the voters on election days.[32] What if such a world had had ATMs? We can imagine the scene:

A dozen dusty commoners are lined up awaiting their turn at the machine when suddenly one of the local gentry, mounted on his blooded stallion, canters into view. As he dismounts, the plain folk shift to one side, remove their hats and avert their eyes. The gentleman strides up to the machine, nodding familiarly to all. Retrieving a great roll of bills from the cash dispenser, he turns, walks back down the line of commoners, and (to display his "liberality") peels off a fresh dollar bill for each of them, receiving in return nods and murmured thanks. Remounting his horse, our gentleman gallops off in a cloud of dust to a hearty "Huzzah!" from the crowd.

Obviously, an absurd scenario ("Of course: every Virginia gentleman knows you send your *footman* to the ATM."), but note your reaction to it. Certainly you'd find it offensive to your values to be in the position of one of the commoners, but would you not find it equally offensive to play the role of the gentleman? Either way, you'd be complicit in a system that presumes that some people have more worth than others.

What makes the scenario work on us is that it takes a familiar practice and shows us how it could be otherwise. Our revulsion at that prospect is an index of our antipathy for being on either end of privilege, and thus an index of how central egalitarian practice is to our values.

From that revulsion I'd take this lesson about how to conduct a "values" discourse in America: We could not view as legitimate any discussion conducted so as to privilege the views of any of the parties.

For a second lesson, let's look at another scenario, not imaginary this time but real (I believe the dateline was Boston, November, 1990.).

freeze-frame:

The ATM and the investment banker

As dusk falls, a motley assortment of tired, just-off-work Americans is standing in line before a row of ATMs, getting money for the upcoming weekend. Up to the adjacent curb pulls the new, sleeker version of the "big" Mercedes, cellular-phone antenna spearing the air. Its door opens, and out steps the very model of sharkdom in his "mine-can-eat-yours" suit. Chirping his car alarm, he turns, notices the line, and his padded shoulders slump. He had tried all day to get his secretary to go down to the machine for him, but there had been no time. Now he knows he'll have to take his place in line with the working stiffs, conform to the same rules as they do, and there's nothing he can do about it.

That sly smile on your lips—what is *that* an index of? If the thought behind your smile is something like *virtue triumphs,* then you believe that this is how life should work in America but too often doesn't.

Or to put it in terms used earlier: This culture was founded on the proposition that everyone is equal in worth, but the hierarchy of wealth and power usually determines who gets respect. What we feel in this scenario is the movement away from "how America is" toward "how America could be if it realized its proposition."

On the strength of your smile I'd propose a second lesson about conducting a "values" discourse in America: We would expect the discussion to be a vehicle for carrying us beyond "what is" in the direction of "what should be."

If our encounter with the ATM reveals specifically American attitudes about a discourse on values, what then did the mining camps teach Royce about "the American character"?

These two qualities then, the *willingness to compromise on matters in dispute,* and *the desire to be in public on pleasant terms with everybody,* worked in the new camps wonders for good order.[33]

Americans' talent for compromise has been noted by many observers. De Tocqueville saw this propensity as one of the chief differences between Europeans and Americans. When Americans wish to promote a cause, he said, they form associations, and so do Europeans. But the American habit is to find that particular way of characterizing the cause that will draw to it the broadest possible support. The European habit is to couch positions in doctrinaire terms so as to narrow the group to only those with militant conviction, for the group's "object is not to convince, but to fight"; "to act, and not to debate."[34] The American with an idea forms a caucus; the European forms "an army."[35]

De Tocqueville says that Americans compromise with each other in order to be able to put together a working majority and thus take power. But I think Royce has his finger on a truer cause: Americans desire to be "on pleasant terms" with each other. On the face of it, this sounds rather namby-pamby, but think of "on pleasant terms" in the mining camp context. You compromise with that guy today because you're going to have to work with him tomorrow. Neither of you is going away. He has as much right to be here as you do.

This is the crux of a specifically American discourse about values. When this building that you're all working on is built, you're all going to have to live with it—and with each other. So you'd better find a solution everybody can live with. One or more of you might be able, by means of your economic or rhetorical power, to gain your will against the wishes of others; and with your power you might even be able to enforce conventions of behavior that will insulate you from the resentment of affected participants. But neither they nor you really believe in those conventions: they fly too much in the face of the equality of worth that is the promise of the common culture all of you share. So all of you in the discourse had better arrive at a result that will let you live "on pleasant terms" with each other. You'd best come up with a charge to the architect that all of you can willingly sign off on.

We've done with the discourse on values what we did with the discourse on results—sharpened our conception of it to the point where a more specific name seems called for. Given Royce's insight about being on good terms, I would suggest *Community* as an appropriate name for a specifically American discourse on values. When we argue over what values a proposed building should embody, our discussion is directed by our belief that even if we aren't, we *should be* a community.

Through Royce's insight we can come to two more lessons: If you will be living with what the Community discourse produces, then that qualifies you to have standing in the discussion to make your views heard there. And the proper "product" of the discourse is the one that can garner the consensus of all who have standing.

With all these lessons in hand, we can get "building-specific" and continue the process of distinguishing the discourses by again answering those four questions about how to conduct the discourse.

In the Community discourse, we are trying to get a building that will embody our values. The work we do in the discourse is to listen to all who will be living with the result we produce. What we are trying to accomplish is a charge to the architect that approaches the ideal of equality of worth for all viewpoints. We will know we are successful when our charge achieves a consensus of the participants.

All that remains now, in our task of distinguishing, is to answer the same questions about the discourse on architectural order. And having renamed the other two, let's follow through and now call this the *Design discourse.*

3

A Way to Think about Practice

If we were to ask our four distinguishing questions about the Design discourse, we'd find that we've already answered three of them: When we speak of a building in the Design discourse, we are trying to get a building that will instance order. The work we do in this discourse is to look for patterns in the charge to the architect, and what we are trying to accomplish is to match the patterns with paradigms of order.

As for the fourth question—how do we judge when our work is successful?—we don't yet know the criterion that tells us we are successful, but I'd like to suggest how success feels: It feels something like an afternoon at the Eames house. That answer sounds a trifle glib, I know, but remember the import we earlier took from the story of that afternoon. What we saw at the Eames house was an exquisite concordance between architecture and domestic ceremonies. But what we felt there was something like, "This is how an architect should conduct all of her life." It was not just design but the vision of a life lived in accord with design that moved us.

It's the validity of that vision of life that I want to argue in this chapter, to say that when properly distinguished, when applied to its proper sphere, design can indeed be a way of living.

In fact it's crucial that we find a way to pay tenable honor to architects' emotions about design as a way to live life. Design epiphanies like mine at the Eames house are, after all, a big part of the reason we became architects. To not account for those emotional ties would leave any theory for practice untrue to the lived reality of architects' lives.

What is required for this link-up of design and life to be tenable is that a single principle be found which can govern both design and life. If we were to possess that principle, we would have the criterion by which to judge success in both the design of buildings and the conduct of life. That principle would disclose the essence of not just good design but *the good life for an architect.*

I use that phrase because it has a precise philosophical implication. It recalls the question Aristotle asked two-and-a-third millenia ago, "What is the good life for Man?" To answer that question, I want to turn again to our explicator of Alberti, Alasdair MacIntyre. The book from which we took that explication, *After Virtue,* is, in its larger purpose, MacIntyre's attempt to show that the only sure escape from modern moral relativism is a critically updated version of Aristotle's answer to that query about the good life.

I will not be adopting the whole of MacIntyre's position, only that part of it which seems to solve our problem of grounding architectural practice in design values—of defining a Design discourse that can speak, in a single voice, of both the building and the architect's life of practice as instantiators of design order.

The key to this dual mode of speaking is in the term *practice.* MacIntyre wants us to think of this term in a quite precise way, so let me give you his definition in full. (A full understanding of this concept will come in a few pages, at which time I hope you'll return to this definition and give yourself the pleasure of contemplating its careful *design.*)

By a "practice" I am going to mean any coherent and complex form of socially established cooperative human activity through which goods internal to that form of activity are realized in the course of trying to achieve those standards of excellence which are appropriate to, and partially definitive of, that form of activity, with the result that human powers to achieve excellence, and human conceptions of the ends and goods involved, are sytematically extended.[1]

Two terms stand out from that definition and cause our incomplete understanding of it: *goods internal to the practice* and *excellence.* Let me define them for you and then return to the characterization of a practice in architectural terms.

MacIntyre draws a distinction between goods internal to the practice and those goods external to it. External goods are easy to define: they are the fame, the power, the wealth that the wider world might shower on us as a result of what we do within our practice. Think of Philip Johnson on the cover of *Time* embracing a six-foot model of his AT&T (now Sony) Building, or (famous to us Bostonians) Rodolfo Machado sporting Gap clothing in a chiaroscuro monochrome advertisement. Clearly the reason the wider world accords such people fame, and its attendant power and money, is rooted in what they have accomplished in design. But are those external goods bestowed out of a comprehending esteem for design excellence?

MacIntyre argues that they are not, and to make the distinction, he invokes the example of a young prodigy involved in another practice, that of chess.[2] He asks us to imagine a young chess player, plucked from his playground world on the basis of observed native talent, being goaded out of his natural playtime amusements by the promise of goods valuable to a child (candy, Nintendo games . . .) for each chess match he wins. Gradually the child matures, to the point where he is sufficiently skilled to command real, wider-world goods.

At that point, for what does the prodigy play? For excellence in strategy and innovation, as recognized by other chess masters? Or for the rewards such excellence can garner from the wider world? He now has the maturity to discriminate between the two, to sense the difference between playing for goods internal to the practice and playing to get those goods external to it. Being able to sense the conflict, his choice now matters ethically: it is encumbent upon him to decide.

But to the wider world watching his play, the two motivations, so crucial within the practice, would be indistinguishable. Is he playing so expertly in order to partake in and advance the excellence of chess, or is he playing for the prize money?

Only the player himself would truly know the answer, but there is another area of endeavor where nearly everyone sees and appreciates the difference between striving for internal versus external goods. The Boston Marathon would not qualify as a practice under MacIntyre's definition, but everyone knows that there are two motivations for running. One is held by perhaps a dozen runners of either sex: they run to win. The other is the motivation of several thousands: they run to finish. The marathon is perhaps the only sporting event where winning is not everything, where not so much victory but excellence is accorded the greatest honor.

The news reports, of course, make a big to-do about who the winners are. That after all is *news,* facts not existing or known before now. That other story—thousands of people running twenty-six miles—was known before the marathon even began, is known in the very mention of the word. No news there. But you have only to watch the congratulations heaped upon ordinary runners to know that finishing is indeed the story that matters, the story people are moved by.

A runner catches the streetcar home after the race, and complete strangers clap her on the back and shake her hand. Another runner drops into a bar and is the hero of the moment, people asking about his time, how it felt, events along the course. In their eyes, excellence in the marathon is in having persevered, in having trained yourself for the challenge, in showing up to confront it and enduring it to the end—goods internal to the practice.

To have the experience of excellence, whether in running or in chess playing—that is the essence of goods internal to the practice. But to say that one can "have" that experience of excellence is to invoke the other sense of having, that of possessing. And in that contrast lies another distinction between internal and external goods.

It's characteristic of external goods that

when achieved they are always some individual's property and possession. Moreover characteristically they are such that the more someone has of them, the less there is for other people. This is sometimes necessarily the case, as with power and fame, and sometimes the case by reason of contingent circumstance as with money. External goods are therefore characteristically objects of competition in which there must be losers as well as winners. Internal goods are indeed the outcome of competition to excel, but it is characteristic of them that their achievement is a good for the whole community who participate in the practice.[3]

So to our chess prodigy who formulates a new strategy, or strings together a series of old strategies in a satisfyingly skillful way, to him belongs the feeling of accomplishment; but the whole community of chess players and the practice of chess itself are enriched by his excellence. When Le Corbusier invented new paradigms of order, when Lutyens played "the high game" of classical order in new ways, that excellence was likewise both possessed and shared. To them, honor for their accomplishment; to us, a practice enriched and renewed. Internal goods for them and for all engaged in the practice.

But to say that we in the practice share in and benefit from achieved excellence is, by implication, to say two more things about internal goods. Goods internal to the practice cannot be *gotten* in any way except by engaging in the practice. (Money, fame, and power, those paradigmatic external goods, can be gotten through any number of pursuits.) And internal goods can be *recognized* and known for what they are only by those who have engaged in the practice.[4] Only practitioners can obtain internal goods, and only they will appreciate them. No one except practitioners can get or "get" goods internal to the practice.

The two points are intimately related: to get internal goods, you have to be able to "get" them. To be able to participate in achieved excellence and use it yourself, you must have an understanding of why it is considered excellent and how it can be applied to achieve further excellence. That understanding of excellence can come only from participation in the practice.

But note that participation in excellence requires not just that you understand why the practice considers something to be excellent, but that you consider it excellent yourself. And to say that you consider something to be excellent is to say that you accept as valid the standards by which the practice judges excellence.

A practice involves standards of excellence and obedience to rules as well as the achievement of goods. To enter into a practice is to accept the authority of those standards and the inadequacy of my performance as judged by them. It is to subject my own attitudes, choices, preferences and tastes to the standards which currently and partially define the practice.[5]

It's vital, when talking about the standards of excellence of the practice of architecture, that we not equate those standards with the ones promulgated by various architectural institutions.

Practices must not be confused with institutions . . . Institutions are characteristically and necessarily concerned with what I have called external goods.

They are involved in acquiring money and other material goods; they are structured in terms of power and status, and they distribute money, power and status as rewards. Nor could they do otherwise if they are to sustain not only themselves but also the practices of which they are the bearers. For no practices can survive for any length of time unsustained by institutions. Indeed so intimate is the relationship of practices to institutions . . . that institutions and practices characteristically form a single causal order in which the ideals and the creativity of the practice are always vulnerable to the acquisitiveness of the institution, in which the cooperative care for common goods of the practice is always vulnerable to the competitiveness of the institution.[6]

So when MacIntyre speaks of "obedience to rules," we are most pointedly not to think immediately of the AIA's *Manual of Practice.* Similarly, we are not to seek in *Progressive Architecture*'s annual design awards the "standards which currently define the practice." We are looking for standards and rules conceived on a more profound basis. And yet there is that phrase, "standards which currently define the practice." How can there be excellence, how can we feel excellence, if the ways in which we judge it can change? That standards do change is undeniable:

Practices never have a goal or goals fixed for all time—painting has no such goal nor has physics—but the goals themselves are transmuted by the history of the activity . . .

To enter into a practice is to enter into a relationship not only with its contemporary practitioners, but also with those who have preceded us in the practice, particularly those whose achievements extended the reach of the practice to its present point. It is thus the achievement, and *a fortiori* the authority, of a tradition which I then confront and from which I have to learn.[7]

But when that "tradition is in good order, it is always partially constituted by an argument about the goods, the pursuit of which gives that tradition its particular point and purpose."[8]

So a tradition of practice is nothing like a "tradition" conventionally conceived. It is an ongoing discussion, a discourse, about what the goals of the practice should be, and what would constitute excellence in the achievement of them. What is "traditional" in this discussion is that "all reasoning takes place within the context of some traditional mode of thought." But that mode of thought itself can change, "transcending through criticism and invention the limitations of what had hitherto been reasoned in that tradition."[9]

So the discussion-that-is-a-practice is possible because at any given time, practitioners share a general conception of what the goals of the practice and excellence in it should be. What keeps the discussion ongoing is invention. What keeps it from going off the rails is criticism.

A satisfying construction, I hope you agree, but one piece is still missing. What began this inquiry was the question of changing standards of excellence. If it is invention that drives the discussion of excellence, and criticism that governs it, then what directs invention? And what conditions criticism?

Before I broach MacIntyre's answer, let me share an insight that might give it point. When I was a child in the 1950s heyday of modernism, when every old building was considered ugly, one style of "oldness" was considered particularly odious—the mansarded houses of the 1870s, those Brown Decades mansions with their dark interiors, painfully tall windows and lugubrious colors. Utter the phrase "haunted house" to a child of the 1950s, and that is the kind of house that would leap into her mind (and probably would to a child of today as well). In 1942 Orson Welles had used such a house to claustrophobic effect in *The Magnificent Ambersons*. And every decade back to the 1880s had its own particular way of seeing in that style a kind of creepy hideousness.

And yet in the 1970s such houses came back into popular esteem. People came to find the colors not gloomy but soothing. Freed of their draperies, the tall windows let in abundant sunlight (and made great places to hang plants). Once revealed by light, the high ceilings with their elaborate moldings invited the eye and the mind up into reaches unimaginable in modern boxlike rooms. By looking at old things in new ways, people were able to find, in those maligned houses, a fit environment for their patterns of habitation and ceremony.

This shift in popular favor is not, of course, serious architectural criticism. But criticism underwent a similar shift, and about some of these very same houses. The way criticism makes its arguments to the practice is by marshalling a group of exemplary buildings and then describing a line that runs, with important variations, through all of them. If such a line extends through time, you have a history. The line is then the "plot" of the story, the buildings strung on the line the "characters." Modernist criticism had threaded such a plot line through certain buildings of the nineteenth and twentieth centuries, and that story gave a coherent, and thus satisfying, explanation of architecture's development in the period.

But to keep a story coherent, you have to limit the number of characters. Some you leave out because they duplicate characters already in the story; others you drop because they are extraneous to the plot or they contradict its thrust. This is not duplicity. No history can cover every single event that has happened in a given period. All that is required is that the events covered be real and that the story explain convincingly about them. The plot-line of modernism's history was "progress toward rationalization," and so the characters cut out of the story were the buildings designed in traditional and newly invented "styles."

One difference, though, between a fictional story and a history is that we never see the characters cut out of a novel and so don't miss them, whereas if historical facts—in our case, buildings—are left out of a history, they stand around and nag at us. And if there are too many of them, or if they seem too important, the story that excludes them might come to seem less than convincing.

Which is precisely what happened to the modernist account. It had told a thrilling story; but to keep believing in it, you had to convince yourself that every "traditional" building was wrongheaded, off the line running through to architecture's destiny. For a while we could believe—and by "we," I mean architects and the public. To all of us, old buildings looked, well, *old*. But when, through a shift in perception, we began to notice those excluded buildings, we were forced to notice as well their *absence* from the story we had believed in, the story which was so convincing that it had conditioned the way we saw the world. Which to were we to believe—the modernist story, or our own perceptions and feelings?

For people like our urban homesteaders moving into their mansarded townhouse, the change in perception presented no great dilemma. Nor did the questions it raised. They had simply discovered themselves to be saying, more and more frequently, "But we *like* old buildings!" And so to their list of "styles we can imagine people liking" they, along with millions of others, added their personal characterization of "Brown Decades." Eighty years of opprobrium wiped out at a stroke.

But for the practice of architecture, the readmission of historical styles was not so simple. Any architect around at the end of the 1960s will remember vividly a feeling of real crisis as the modernist story as told by Pevsner and Giedion seemed to become, almost daily, less and less convincing. It was as if the rug had been pulled out from under us and beneath it was—no floor.

But the crisis was resolved, and the resolution was accomplished in the telling of other stories. Critics and historians began gradually to trace new lines through the canon of buildings, including, this time, those buildings excised by modernism. They sketched new plotlines in which those characters now had consequential roles. Of course, in the tracing of those new lines, plot coherence required that star billing be rearranged: in the new stories, some of modernism's major players became mere walk-ons, and a few were dropped from the cast entirely. But if that's what it takes to get a convincing story of what we do and why we do it, then so be it.

For all its metaphor slippage about "plot" and "characters," there are important points to be drawn from this story of both popular and critical history being written and rewritten. The first point is that no mode of architecture that is pursued seriously for a period of time is likely to be judged forever as a mistake. Not the Brown Decades, certainly not modernism in its various forms, and (I would bet) not even the High Glitz postmodernism of the 1980s. All will eventually be included in the family of respectable architecture. And their inclusion will come by means of new critical histories, stories in which a formerly denigrated mode now plays a central part.

In the interest of plot coherence, those new inclusive histories will themselves exclude from their stories buildings and modes that previous histories had included. We thus might have before us stories about the same era in time, or about the same phenomena, that are quite different from each other. But such histories can coexist with each other. They will in fact have to coexist, as no single story can include within itself all that has been built and thought.

This might sound, on the face of it, like a rather shaky basis on which to found a practice of architecture. But in MacIntyre's thought is a principle that not only makes the system cohere as a practice, but links the system to the lived life of the architect. The principle is *narrative continuity*. Let me explain.

We saw that plot coherence—"narrativity"—was what made criticism convincing. MacIntyre reminds us that the same narrativity is what convinces us that our *lives* are being lived purposefully, meaningfully. If we can see an action we take in life as extending a story we are living, we will think that action consistent with something larger than itself alone. We will think of that action as purposive in terms of *extending* that story, and meaningful in terms of *being explained by* that story.

Similarly, when we are faced with a decision about what action to take, we would have the most confidence in that action which seemed to extend a story we had lived successfully thus far. We would anticipate that that action, once completed, would give us the feeling of purpose and meaning we feel about actions viewed retrospectively.

And yet we have all experienced acts we have done that seem to contradict the stories we imagine ourselves to be living. Such actions nag at us, asking for an explanation. And so when some unexpected insight discloses to us a line on which that action seems to have a place, we willingly grab it, and entertain the possibility of imagining ourselves living a story different from the one we had thought ourselves to be living.

In order to have all our actions strung on plot-lines, in order to have no action left estranged from a narrative and thus unaccounted for (and sensing from experience the impossibility of a single narrative encompassing all our actions), we accept the concept of our living out coexistent narratives. If they overlap (as they usually will) and we find some actions "narrated" in more than one way, we accept that as the price we must pay for finding a home in a story for every one of our actions.[10]

Living out multiple narratives is one of those existential conditions of our lives. And because we accept that condition in our lives, we're prepared by that experience to find multiple, overlapping criticisms satisfying in our practice.

Which is to say: the principle by which we aspire to conduct and explain our lives convinces us as the principle by which to conduct our practice. And vice versa. A single principle for both—which raises the possibility that life and practice might be a single, almost undifferentiated set of stories, life and design alike conducted to the principle of narrative continuity.

For MacIntyre, the life lived with narrative continuity *is* the good life. To the extent that narrative continuity names what so compels us about the lives of Ray Eames and Frank Lloyd Wright, then to that extent is it the principle behind the good life for an architect.

What remains now is to fulfill the promise made in the introduction, that this theory for practice would not entail a whole new way of conducting practice and life, but would instead be a way of making sense of what we architects already do. I've made the bold proposition that narrative continuity is the principle by which to conduct life, design, and criticism. Whether this principle makes a kind of sense of your life, only you can judge (although I sincerely hope it does). But ask yourself, as you read the following schema, if this doesn't accord with design and criticism as you know it.

From history and criticism (and as we practice long, from our own careers seen critically) we get narratives that disclose to us paradigms of order. These stories are built on narrative lines, which can be of several kinds. One commonly used line is *building type*—churches, say. Through a collection of churches we might thread a line based on how they handle light, or how they focus attention on the altar, or how they accommodate the congregation. Each of the intersections of through-line and building would yield paradigms of order (for light, the high clerestory and the rose window; for focus, the altar, the axis of the nave, and the raised platform backed by a screen; for seating, ranked box pews or concentric benches or balconies and galleries).

Or the line running through might be a *building purpose* stated more abstractly. Our look, in a previous chapter, at "buildings meant to effectuate a result" yielded a narrative about a saltworks, a paupers' workhouse, and a hospital. When those buildings were strung together, a plot-line we can call "organizational schema" thrust itself to our attention. And when we looked at the buildings in that way, we saw, in the case of the hospital, the ordering paradigm of "functional blocks clipped onto a linear spine." From that paradigm, taken as a new theme, we could have spun other connecting lines through yet other buildings.

By looking at architecture's history through the lens of any of these narrative lines, an architect is presented with a number of paradigmatic solutions to the recurring problem of how to order form.

Imagine a charge to the architect that might have come out of that kitchen-table discussion described in the previous chapter. If the architect apprehended from that discussion the pattern "several children each wanting very different bedrooms," she might have characterized that pattern, to herself, as the paradigm of order "different blocks clipped onto a common spine." Her adopting that paradigm as a way to accommodate the children's bedrooms would be not just a design solution, though; it would be a proposal to an imagined history for a plot-line that would connect her use of the paradigm with its analogous use in other buildings—our Royal Victoria Hospital for example, or each side of the University of Virginia Lawn, and many others. The full meaning of her design act would then be not just the meaning it held for the children and the family. There would be the meaning of the act for her in the practice, told in the stories that the world of criticism might spin from among all the uses of that paradigm, including hers.

The use of each paradigm in our building thus has a potential narrative continuity with other uses of that paradigm. And following the same principle, we see to it that the paradigms in our building have a narrative continuity with each other.

So the practice of architectural design works like this: Criticism and history thread narrative lines through buildings and their various aspects. Those narratives reveal to us paradigms of order, which we then use in our designs—giving to criticism and history yet other buildings through which they can thread yet other plot-lines. And when they do, they will reveal yet more (or differently seen) paradigms of order for yet further use.

We live our professional lives within this ever-permuting series of narratives, for which we architects supply the characters, which history and criticism then use to fashion stories. Excellence in the practice is thus adjudged to have occurred when a particular design act can be "enstoried," when history and criticism can contrive plot-lines in which that design act plays a significant role. So we architects practice so as to produce buildings that might achieve such narrative inclusion—either by contriving for our building a place in a narrative already written, or one we see as nascent, or a narrative not yet imagined but tenably possible.

How though does this model for practice connect with *life*? The answer lies in our design act of matching patterns of living with paradigms of order. As designers we believe that we make proposals for design excellence when we accommodate a client's living pattern in an ordering paradigm. By that matching we connect our design act with critical-historical narratives (existent, nascent, or imagined) and thus achieve, in our minds, excellence. We additionally hope that our clients will apprehend something of this connection themselves and thus see their living patterns as having the potential for more profound meaning than they had imagined.

In the places we architects contrive *for ourselves,* though, we serve as our own clients, matching our existent living patterns with paradigms of order we esteem, proposing our own lives and their paradigm-matched surroundings as participants in ongoing critical narratives, and thus gaining for ourselves a feeling of achieved excellence.

But we architects, uniquely, have the ability—even propensity—to run the matching process in reverse. As designers we hold in our heads the full panoply of paradigms of order and the narratives of which they are a part. But certain of those narratives we regard with more favor—to wit, the ones in which we imagine our own practices to participate. If you gain participation in a narrative by matching a living pattern with a paradigm revealed in that narrative, then you can either match a paradigm to a living pattern (as we do with clients) or you can match a living pattern to a paradigm. Because of how important it is to us to participate in those narratives, we architects willingly bend our living patterns so as to effectuate a plausible connection between them and a paradigm of order we esteem. We gladly, almost unconsciously, change our patterns of living so that they will accord with, and thus be imaginably matched to, esteemed paradigms of order and their associated critical-historical narratives.

We work the system of practice backward, determining to make our lives match paradigms of order, and in that determination to give our lives and surroundings a feeling of continuity with the critical-historical narratives we most believe in.

That is what our just-graduated architect was doing when he chose only those two perfect chairs. That's what Ray Eames and Frank Lloyd Wright did. It's what, in her own way, your teacher did. And it's what the architects at the AIA convention were doing. It is how you achieve for your work and your life the excellence shown to us by the narratives of our practice. And again, for an architect, this conformance of life to paradigm is not an onerous task but a positive joy. It is the good life for an architect.

We're now in a position to answer that last question about the Design discourse. We said earlier that when we are speaking in the Design discourse, we are trying to get a building that will instance order. The work we do in the discourse is to look for patterns in the charge to the architect, and what we are trying to accomplish is to match the patterns with paradigms of order. We know we are successful when our design has narrative continuity with the histories of our practice as revealed by criticism.

So we now have a sense of how the three discourses think about the building. What we have to do next is to see how these three different ways of thinking can work together actually to produce the building.

4

Working with Other Ways of Thinking

Every architect knows that the process by which a building gets pro-
grammed, designed, built, and occupied is nothing like a neat and
tidy flow chart. The lines of decision split, turn back on themselves,
and sometimes just dissolve as the building lurches from idea to reality. Yet we're able to navigate the process, and the reason we can is
that we have a conceptual framework for understanding it. We have
in our heads a simple idea about how the process works as a whole,
and with that idea we're able to judge whether any particular circumstance in the real transaction moves the process forward in accord
with the ideal or impedes it; and if it impedes, then its difference
from the ideal will tell us *how* it's impeding and what we might do to
nudge the process back onto course.

Most architects take their idealized conceptual framework from
the standard contracts the AIA promulgates to govern the relationships among architect, owner, and contractor in the design and construction process. What I want to do here is to propose an alternative
conceptual framework, one that idealizes the process as a transaction
among the three discourses, the three ways of thinking about the
building.

The framework will be idealized in these senses:

• It will personify the discourses, treat each as if it were an actual
group of people who thought about the building only and purely in

the way of that discourse. I'll be doing this as a shorthand, for we know full well that no real person or group thinks or speaks from only a single, narrow perspective (even if they might *present* such an image, for strategic purposes). Each of us operates in multiple worlds, and because of that we learn to see things from multiple perspectives. And for those worlds we don't operate in habitually, most of us are capable of at least partial empathy for a "foreign" perspective.

It would be a rare community activist who was wholly incapable of seeing things through an entrepreneur's eyes, and vice versa—and a poor architect who couldn't think like both. People who see things differently are able to converse with each other, and they do. But when they extend toward each other, each does so from the base of his own perspective. So for the sake of clarity, in the idealized model, each discourse will see things in only its own way.

• The conceptual framework will also be idealized in that it will break the process into discrete, sequential stages. In a real building project, not only do portions of the work elide into each other, the process often backtracks so that steps get repeated. Again for the sake of clarity—to give us that ideal compass to navigate by—our process will proceed smoothly through its parts from start to finish.

With those cautions in place, I can present how the model works. In the course of a building project, three distinct types of work get done:

• At the end of the project, when the building is completed and has been occupied for some time, comes the *judgmental work,* when the three discourses get a sense of whether the building has achieved fulfillment of their expectations.

• At the start of the process comes the *synthetic work.* This is when the Community and Market discourses formulate the charges that each will make to the architect. Equally synthetic is the work Design does in response to the charges—finding patterns and matching them with paradigms of order.

• Between these two stages comes the *transactional work,* those conversations between Design in the person of the architect and each of the two other discourses about how well the developing design is responding to the charge each made.

Each of these kinds of work has its own modalities, its own standards of judgment, even its own language. It is in fact these differences, rather than their sequence in time, that most differentiates them: in reality any two or even all three might occur simultaneously. So let's look at them in detail, in this same sequence.

The judgmental work

Let's first remind ourselves of what each discourse is judging. The Market perspective is looking to discover whether, with the building now in operation, marketplace substitution has happened. Now that they are inhabiting it, Community members are asking among themselves whether the building feels like an embodiment of their consensus about values. And Design is looking toward the first critical reactions to the building for some indication of whether the building will be included in historical narratives.

All well and good, but what does it mean to say that "a discourse will be judging"? Exactly what persons will be doing this judging? Upon what factors will these judgments be rendered? Clearly we are talking here not about the work of an actual tribunal, rather a determination more akin to those presumptive decisions characterized as "public opinion"—a phrase whose meaning could be stated, "The rough consensus of people who think about this issue seems to be . . . "

So in the case of the Market discourse, we are talking about the "judgment" made by the people to whom the building in question is directed. Did the big law firm in town relocate into the new office building? Did the trendsetters switch their allegiance to the new restaurant? Did allergy patients see sufficient difference to transfer their therapy to the new clinic?

For the Community discourse, when the building was finally erected, did local preservation groups feel that the new building accorded with the look and feel of the neighborhood as they conceived it? Did the local advocacy groups—for handicapped, environmental, traffic, and community morality issues—feel that the building advanced their particular agendas? The people who work in the building had an image of how they might ideally interact during their days there; does the building as built foster the living out of that image?

And for the Design discourse, what sorts of commentary have appeared in the press? Did the architecture critic of the local paper comment favorably? Did the building get picked up by *P/A* or *Record* or *Architecture?*—and if so, was it in a feature article or just a news blurb? And was the tenor of the commentary that the building had "broken new ground" on an issue of long standing? That it had offered a new interpretation of an enduring theme in design? That it was a significant advance in the development of the oeuvre of its architect?

That's *who* is judging. Before we consider the basis on which these judgments are rendered, though, we can say at least two things about them.

• First, such judgments are provisional. Any or all of them might be reversed in the future. The Market, after initial acceptance, might later be temped elsewhere, by somebody else's offerings. Community's images of fittingness or correctness or interaction might change in the future, leaving our building the embodier of discredited values. And the consensus of critical commentary about our building might shift as standards of criticism change. (I am old enough to recall the magazines' adulation of Minoru Yamasaki; I'm young enough that I might still be around when his "romantic modernism" is re-appreciated, likely on a basis that would be unthinkable to us now.)

• It's also plain that such judgments will be equivocal. They will be a mix of "yes" and "no" determinations on the whole work, interweaved with a collection of judgments on aspects of the building with the tenor "on the one hand, yes; but on the other hand, no."

A slippery situation, granted; but does it not reflect the way in which consensus about a contentious issue is always and inevitably worked out over time? It is the world we architects work in.

But equally a part of the world architects work in is the manner in which the bases for these judgments are set. It's clear that the charge to an architect does not come divided cleanly into Market concerns and Community concerns. In practice, the architect receives a charge that is a mix of those (and indeed other) concerns. But remember that we are idealizing here, to gain a compass through that tangled thicket. Having these two categories in our head allows us to discriminate, to separate out instances of each concern from the mix and then treat each in a manner consonant with its agenda. Without that discrimination, we're liable to find ourselves, as the architects of the first chapter did, misreading those concerns and dealing with them in a wholly inappropriate manner.

If it seems a useful fiction to think of us architects as receiving two separate charges from the Community and Market discourses, let me then extend that fiction to say that an architect receives a third charge to which she must respond, the charge from the Design discourse.

So in this idealized conception of practice, the architect labors to address three different charges, to produce a building that all three discourses will judge (in the rough way they do) to have achieved the conception of fulfillment that each of them holds.

But this idea of fulfilling a charge immediately raises a question. The minds that set the Market charge are not themselves the marketplace, they are merely stand-ins for that larger phenomenon, making their best guesses about what the marketplace will decide. If the architect's building addresses their charge perfectly and yet fails to achieve marketplace substitution, is that the architect's "fault"?

Similarly for the mind-sets we are calling the Community discourse. The people speaking those concerns are likewise stand-ins for the much larger community of users and affected parties. Their charge to the architect is likewise a best guess about the larger community's propensities and perceptions. If the architect meets their charge and yet the building fails to engender a feeling of embodiment, is that the architect's "fault"?

And similarly too for the Design discourse. The architect herself is the "stand-in" here; she is speaking (to herself) for the larger critical community. The charge she sets herself is her best guess about how some portion of the present (or imagined) critical world will view her work. If her work fails to garner the hoped-for inclusion in critical narratives, is that the "fault" of the architect?

All this talk of "fault" suggests that we might look to real, legal liability for insights into these questions of responsibility. Think for a moment about the similarities and differences between these questions:

- The roof leaks. Is it the architect's fault?
- The building fails to rent. Is it the architect's fault?
- The community doesn't feel the building speaks their values. Is it the architect's fault?
- Critics and historians haven't included the building in their narratives. Is it the architect's fault?

What we often forget, when looking at legal liability, is that the question at the core of liability litigation is not, "When an unpredicted or unwanted result occurs, to whom can blame be assigned?" What's more truly being judged in a liability case is whether one party has a responsibility to another and if so, whether he has done those things that would discharge the responsibility.

"Discharge" is the operative word here. The real question we are asking here is not "What responsibility for consequences does the architect owe the three discourses?" but rather, "What must she do to *no longer owe* them?" If the architect in the first of our questions had specified a recognized roofing system, and if her construction details had conformed to accepted practice, then (in fair courts) she would have discharged her obligation and should be free of fault for the leak. Similarly for "liability" to the discourses in the other three questions. If the architect had truly met the formulated mandates of the three discourses (including those Design mandates she had formulated for herself), she would have discharged her responsibility to them. What we are looking for here is a standard of *ethical closure* on the matter of meeting the charges from the discourses.

We can perhaps better understand the difference between this "ethical closure of responsibility for the charge" and "legal liability for the building" by remembering Macintyre's distinction between a practice and the institutions in which it operates. His insight reminds us that there is the judgment of excellent behavior within the practice, and then there is the determination of accountability for reprehensible behavior in the institution. Ethical closure is a concept of the practice; discharge of liability is a fact of institutions. The two may touch at some points, but they are by no means the same. To achieve one is not to achieve the other.

It seems tenable to say that ethical closure is achieved when all three discourses agree that the design of the building has provided a full address to the whole of each of the charges. Closure comes at this point because it is at this moment that the stand-ins for the three discourses can say to themselves, "Yes, I think this design will achieve fulfillment as I see it. I am prepared to offer this up for judgment by the larger world of people who think along these lines."

In terms of this idealized model then, the architect's ethical responsibility *opens* with the formulation of the charge in the synthetic work, and it *closes* with the satisfaction of the charge at the end of the transacting phase. That signing-off then opens the construction of the building—which we conceptualize here as the direct translation of the design into built reality. In this model, construction is seen as a pause between stages of the process; at the conclusion of construction, when the building is up and running in the world, then commences the time of the judgmental work.

There is an ironclad obligation that the architect must assume in this model (it is the ethical trade-off for achieving discharge of responsibility for the final result). In this system it is incumbent on the architect to make certain, through all the presentations she makes, that the transacting parties have a full understanding of the building they are signing off on. If they are not seeing the same building the architect is about to send into construction, their decision to endorse the building lacks an ethical basis. That is, each of the three discourses at the moment of signing-off is making a prediction that *this building we are imagining* will achieve fulfillment when it is presented to the larger world: those predictions will matter only if it is indeed *the building we imagined* that is actually presented.

Clearly too it is important that the charge to the architect be formulated not just in detail, but that it truly convey those characteristics that each discourse considers crucial to the achievement of its idea of fulfillment. It's the task of the synthetic work to ensure this precision and authenticity.

The synthetic work

The work of this phase is synthetic in that for all of the discourses it involves wrapping parts in wholes. Each of the discourses, though, does its work in a different way.

• The charge from Design—the charge the architect makes to himself—would naturally take the form of a global statement about his desires for the whole building and a series of statements about its parts and aspects. To produce a synthesis that can encompass all that, Design thinking would typically work both *from the whole to the parts* and *from the parts to the whole*.

• The Market discourse, by contrast, will usually set its charge to the architect by working *from the whole to the parts*. The marketing strategy for achieving substitution will be settled upon first, and from that whole the marketers will derive the component parts they think are needed to make it fly in the marketplace.

• Community usually works from the other direction, *from the parts to the whole*. Typically, each participant in the process will have a vision about some part or aspect of the building; it is the vision of the whole that must be hammered out in discussion.

How, though, do the discourses actually accomplish their respective syntheses?

Design's synthetic work

Let's admit, right up front, that no architect is going to work in the way a strict reading of this model of practice would suggest: First he puts on his Design discourse hat and formulates a charge—a strategy for achieving Design excellence—which he writes down and passes over to the architect. He then removes his Design hat, slides over one seat, puts on his architect's hat, reads through the charge and *only then* starts about the task of conceiving a building that will meet the charge from Design.

Architects know that we formulate our strategies for excellence *as* we imagine and try out design concepts: we critique our developing concepts by holding them up for comparison with conceptions of excellence we have internalized from our readings of history and criticism. In choosing a concept we propose it as acceptable to those standards and thus includable within them as an "examplar" or "challenger" or "reinterpreter" of those standards.

Confusing? See if this doesn't make sense: Think of an architect's design concept as having both an explicit and an implicit nature. Explicitly, it is a response to the charges from Community and the Market, a configuration of form that encompasses their desires and priorities. But implicit in the concept is a charge from Design, that conception of excellence that the architect developed for himself in the imagining of the concept. Even though he conceived it himself, and even if he never voiced it in so many words, he will view that conception of excellence as a charge he feels obligated to fulfill. That the conception, and thus the charge, will change during the design process does not vitiate the obligation: each concept, in its turn, will speak a Design charge to the architect.

So if an architect's design concept has this dual nature—explicit response to Community and Market, implicit response to Design— how does an architect move from a client's program to a design concept? Many people have tried to analyze the process, some even to systematize it. And though each attempt has given us architects useful insights into what we do, none of the analyses has proved so comprehensive or compelling as to win wide acceptance. Perhaps this is because architects view their design methods as too personal, too unique to each of them, to be generalized about. Perhaps the process of design synthesis really is, as some suspect, ineffable, not comprehensively explainable at all.

I do, though, think it's fair to say that almost every architect's design process has something to do, as we said earlier, with finding patterns within the charges from the discourses and then matching them with conceptions of order. That's the "parts-to-whole" work. But the architect's first ideas of order, his initial "wholes," will never be comprehensive, never able to encompass all of the contents of the charges. So the architect will then have to work from his provisional wholes back to the parts, seeing if those unencompassed parts will look different—that is, encompassable—if they are viewed in the ways the provisional wholes suggest. Inevitably this new look will reveal patterns not previously seen, new potential wholes, and these new perceptions will begin the process anew.

What prevents this loop from being endless is the architect's ability to stop the iterations and settle upon a conception of wholeness. Once that happens, regardless of how it happens, the architect has a design concept and is ready to move from synthesis to transaction— trying out the concept on the Market and Community stand-ins for their reaction—which in all but the most fortuitous cases will occasion a return to the synthesis mode.

The Market's synthetic work

Luckily for our analysis, the Market's synthetic work is both well understood and pretty straightforward. It's easy for us to imagine the process by which entrepreneurs might concoct a marketing strategy for a store or office or clinic, and from it derive the features needed to make that strategy work.

It's also easy to imagine how those requisite features would be communicated to the architect—as a series of named and described facilities, with operational requirements for each.

As simple as this seems, it's important to keep in mind that the charge to the architect from the Market is not simply, "Provide the listed facilities operating as mandated." Each of those facilities and procedures has a role in the overall marketing strategy, and so each can be fully understood only by reference to the whole strategy.

Just as was the case with Design, the parts here can be understood only by reference to the whole, and the whole can be understood only by reference to the parts.

Community's synthetic work

But if it's easy to imagine how the Market works from the whole of the marketing strategy to its parts, it's much harder to imagine how Community works toward its whole of a consensus vision.

We know at least what the "parts" are: they are the views of individuals and groups about the building and portions or aspects of it. To get a sense of how a consensus from among such views might be formed, I'd like to have you listen in on a Community discourse where consensus *wasn't* reached, and hear an astute observer explain how it could have happened.

The observer is Daniel Kemmis in his capacity as mayor of Missoula, Montana. The discourse is a public hearing in Missoula about a proposed regional land-use plan, a discourse thus very much about what sorts of values should be embodied in a shared setting.

To feel the import of the story, you need to be aware of the particular place Missoula occupies in the mind of the people of Montana. Home to the state university (and a distinguished writing program that included Norman Maclean of *A River Runs Through It* fame), Missoula has long been seen by rural interests as a hotbed of radical ideas and effete lifestyles. And, there being a grain of truth in that perception, town folk harbor converse feelings about the farmers and ranchers around them.

So at the hearing it was not surprising that

the rural residents spoke passionately of their property rights and of their undying opposition to the urban arrogance which would presume to limit those rights in any way. The city dwellers who supported the plan spoke just as passionately of the quality of life which was so important to them and the need they felt for some regulations to protect that quality of life against the developments which threatened it.[1]

An explanation of what was going on at that hearing is provided by the researchers at the Harvard Negotiation Project. In their book *Getting to Yes* they draw a distinction between *interests* and *positions*.[2] Interests correspond to what we have been calling *values*. They express what really matters to us. Values are in fact the means we use to decide *what* matters to us, and how much. Positions, on the other hand, are *strategies*. We look down the road at the people we're going to be negotiating with, and the forum in which the negotiation will be held, and we fabricate the position that we think will best advance our interests, or in some cases, counter theirs.

Kemmis's hearing participants clearly were strategizing, the tactic of each group being to portray its position as rooted in a great and venerable ideology—the town people invoking "quality of life" to bolster their position, the rural folk utilizing an appeal to "property rights." But once we are aware of this distinction between positions and values, we can see that a public hearing, dealing only with the positions voiced before it, often slights the unvoiced values that lie behind the positions. Why?

If we were to imagine a band of "decision space" between the positions of any two parties, then "fairness" might be that policy which occupied the midpoint of the space, the classic example being a negotiation over the price of some item for sale in which the seller and buyer split the difference between their offers. But for such an averaging to achieve fairness, it would have to be the case that the seller had highballed her asking price to an extent roughly equal to how much the buyer had lowballed his offer. If the buyer were truly to express what the item was worth to him (its *value* according to his values) while the seller vastly inflated her asking price, then the whole decision space would shift toward the seller; and splitting the difference would achieve nothing like fairness to the values of the parties.

But consider the situation that exists at real hearings which deal with issues much more complex than simple price. There the two parties, anticipating each others' moves, might well formulate positions at some considerable distance from their true values. If we were to imagine the band of decision space between *these* positions, we'd likely find the two parties' true values mapped entirely outside that band. And so when the hearing officers split the difference by picking the midpoint between the parties' voiced positions, the "fairness" that would be achieved between positions might be nothing like fairness to the participants' values, which are after all what really matter to them.

Such a situation is clearly what Kemmis's hearing participants were setting themselves up for. Under the pressure of the hearing format, each group had voiced a position not just at variance from its true values but actually inimical to them. Listening to their arguments, you might reasonably have concluded that each group devoutly desired that the other group would simply go away, the townspeople preferring to be surrounded by open wilderness to assure them "quality of life," the rural folk wishing to be freed from the town and all its restrictions on their "property rights."

But from long experience Kemmis knows these people, and he knows that neither group at the hearing truly wished for the implications of its voiced position to come to pass. He knew that

if one were to ask most of the people from outside Missoula why they lived where they did, and if they could be persuaded to speak honestly, they would talk not only about living on some particular piece of land in the country but also about living within driving distance of a town like Missoula . . . And the same would be true of the Missoulians: part of the quality of their lives depends upon their living surrounded by rural land and rural living.[3]

If either group had seen its implicit "go away" position triumph in the hearing, it would have seen what it valued irreparably damaged. And if the hearing had promulgated a midpoint policy between the two voiced positions, that policy's effects on the participants' values would have been almost completely unpredictable.

Why would otherwise reasonable people act this way?

The crux of the problem lies in the format of the public hearing, or more particularly, in the position of the hearing officer. As long as there are hearing officers whose job it is to speak the common interest, no one of the participants in a hearing will attempt to speak a vision of a common interest: that is not *your* role but the role of the proceedings themselves. Besides, to do so would be to surrender whatever strategic advantage your fabricated position might offer you before the hearing officer. You would be in the position of the bargainer who states what he really is prepared to pay—a patsy. And worse: as long as the participants put out false reports of their values, the hearing officers attempting to split the difference between positions will be adjudicating on an untrue basis.

I've spent all this time criticizing the public hearing format not out of any particular animus against it but because it is the model many of my fellow architects adopt, unwittingly, to deal with their versions of the Community discourse. If you are an architect, you know the drill: each of the groups with a stake in the design of the building submits to you a list of their "needs," which you then attempt to bring to resolution in your design.

But we can see now that those "needs" will likely have been strategically distorted, so that even if the architect were to achieve a truly "disinterested" resolution of them, his resolution would have a false basis and thus would affect the values hidden behind the positions in ways he could never know.

And more: it is unlikely that our architect would actually have reached his resolution on a truly disinterested, value-free basis (if such a thing is even possible). More likely he would have chosen that resolution which best accorded with Design values.

The architect's design would be a resolution, on an inauthentic basis, of misrepresented interests—surely an untenable method for achieving a consensus among the diverse interests (values) of a community of building users.

It's vital that Community's consensus not be fashioned for it but that its participants synthesize it themselves, along authentic Community lines. Kemmis's reading of the hearing shows us something of the character of such a consensus when it is authentically arrived at. Listen to his full analysis of the hearing.

What I did not hear was any sense of how these people's fates were woven together, how the good life that they each wanted depended upon the others being secured in a different but equally good life. It seemed to me likely that if one were to ask most of the people from outside Missoula why they lived where they did, and if they could be persuaded to speak honestly, they would talk not only about living on some particular piece of land in the country but also about living within driving distance of a town like Missoula. Missoula, in other words, is part of the place they had chosen to live—not an accidental but an integral part. And the same would be true of the Missoulians: part of the quality of their lives depends upon their living surrounded by rural land and rural living. They have a stake in that rural life; they have a stake in its being a good life.

I heard, that evening, almost no expression of that mutual stake in the shape of one another's lives.[4]

There was indeed a consensus, but it was hidden from the participants by the modalities of argumentation forced on them by the hearing process. There was an unrecognized consensus about a good life in the region which each group lived separately but which—to continue to be good—depended on the members of the other group being in place, living their different but complementary lives.

But more than a common way of living linked these people. They also inhabited a common environment, and that fact is crucial for our analysis. Kemmis reminds us of the etymological root of that word *inhabit*. In a century-long process of living together, town dwellers and rural folk had evolved *habits* of living that felt good because they felt in concordance with the qualities of the region as a whole.[5]

We've encountered that term *concordance* before. It was the characteristic that led us architects to experience design epiphanies in places like Wright's Taliesins and the Eames house. There too we felt the presence of a concordance between values about how to live and the surroundings in which the inhabitants lived that life. And we further said that when such a concordance is present, we feel that our values about living are embodied in our surroundings.

So, unvoiced among the inhabitants of the Missoula region was the recognition that together they daily experienced a kind of continuing design epiphany in their shared region of Montana. Their ways of living had evolved into such a concord with their surroundings that when they looked at those surroundings, they found their values about *the good life in the Missoula region* embodied there.

The had achieved Community's concept of fulfillment in a setting, but in reverse: in Montana the setting had come first, the values after. Nevertheless, if the inhabitants could have been brought to speak their common vision of life in the region, that statement would have spoken their consensus on what values a *fulfilling* setting would embody.

Kemmis's analysis shows that the Community discourse will reach its consensus when each participant can speak a vision of a common inhabitation (or hear it spoken) in such terms that she can imagine ways in which that vision describes what matters in her life. We can surmise that such a statement will need to be multivalent and ambiguous, perhaps even poetic, for it to garner consensus.

But it need not be meaningless. As was the case with the Market discourse, the whole and the parts of a Community consensus make complete sense only when seen in reference to each other. Each of the part desires of the participants would condition and focus the ambiguity of the consensus vision. To hear all the part desires would be to come to a full and nuanced understanding of the consensus vision of inhabitation.

If I have not been able to make all of this clear to you, hold on for a while. Chapter 5 will present a concrete instance of part feelings about inhabitation and their resolution in a statement at first poetic but later comprehensible through reference to its parts.

In the meantime, we need to address the question of how such part feelings, and the consensus they comprise, can be conveyed to the architect in the form of a charge to which the architect can respond.

The transactional work

Remember what is going on in this, the phase that sets the design of the building. Even though they are transacting with each other about the building, all of the discourses are looking down the road toward its judgment by their respective like-minded portions of the larger world. While working with the architect, the Market is looking to see that it gets a building likely to achieve substitution, and Community wants out of the architect a building likely to embody its hard-won consensus vision of living, whereas Design wants the architect to produce a building that might come to be included in historical narratives.

What's an architect to do in such a situation?

Let me propose a visualization of what is going on here. Imagine two circles partially overlapping, the right-hand circle representing the Design discourse, the left-hand circle either of the other two discourses. Say that the overlap zone represents any *design act* by the architect, from the smallest detail up to the complete building. The full circles would then represent how each discourse *sees* that design act.

In response to a part of the charge from the Market, there might be, in the overlap area, the design act of an arrangement of sales counters, which Design would see as an instance of architectural order and the Market would see as facilities needed for its marketing strategy. Similarly for transactions about the whole charge from the Market, with a proposed design for the whole building now occupying the overlap: whereas the Market discourse would evaluate the design for its potential to achieve substitution in the marketplace, Design would see there a bid for the building's inclusion in historical narratives.

But to imagine replaying this paragraph and substituting the analogous Community terms—that makes us realize once again that our understanding of the Market comes easy while understanding of Community comes hard. We have a sense of what happens when Community and Design consider the whole building—Design looks for inclusion in narratives, Community for embodiment of its consensus—but what are the *parts* that both look at? What is analogous, in the Community discourse, to "a component part of the marketing strategy" in the Market discourse?

Since we seem to know it better, let's try to answer the question by analogizing from the Market discourse to the Community discourse. When the Market charged the architect with providing that sales counter, the charge might have come in the form of "so many lineal feet of . . . " But such a charge would be the Market doing some of the architect's work. The real charge behind that preemptive specification would have been more like, "*That* (that design act) should *accomplish this result.*"

Now, it's important to note that if the result to be accomplished is "selling *X* volume of cosmetics," that result can be accomplished in many ways. But the ways that are potentially *right* are the ones that accord with the Market's larger goals, up to and including its total goal for the building itself, that marketing strategy.

If that is so, then the analogous charge Community makes is, "*That* (that design act) should *feel like this.*" And by further analogy, there would be many ways to bring about that feeling, but the right ones would be those that accorded with Community's overall vision of shared inhabitation.

So the question we need to answer, if we are to have a way of translating Community's values talk into Design's order talk, is this: What descriptor of "feeling like that" would isolate out a set of possibilities, from which Design and Community could then choose one on the basis of its potential concordance with their larger goals? For an answer, let's return to Montana.

In the inhabitants' imagined conversation about living in concord with their surroundings was the implication that elsewhere, beyond that region, there were surroundings where that concord was *not* felt. We can speculate that at some distance from Missoula, people didn't use the town as part of their lives, and so their habits wouldn't be those town-and-country patterns of the people at the hearing. So even if the inhabitants couldn't exactly describe the qualities of the region that made them feel concord there, they could doubtless point to places where they *didn't* feel it.

Numerous commentators have remarked on this sense of "being inside" a special place. For my purposes I want to call this feeling of being-within a *here-there sense*—a feeling that *here* is distinct from *there*. The feeling exists at all sorts of scales. We can be sure that the Missoulians, when thinking of their town, felt a sense of *here* (the town) being distinct from the country around, a feeling that the country folk would have felt in reverse, their *here* being the open spaces around the town.

You can imagine feeling *here* about your farm, your block, your house, your room, and on down to your chair. (Our imagined client who placed the wing chair in the white room did so to establish a *here* distinct from the *there* of his architect-designed room.)

We might say that a *here-there* sense is the basal condition of the Community discourse: you have to feel that there *is* a place distinct from another, different place before you can feel that a place embodies your values. The leap I want to make here is to say that there are different species of this *here-there* sense, and that their difference lies in the differences we can feel in the relationship between *here* and *there*. If we can arrive at a characterization of those different relationship feelings, then we might have a way for Community to charge the architect, in (idealized) words like these: "Show me design acts that engender this particular *here-there* feeling. Then we can decide which of those possibilities accord with our vision of inhabitation, and which accord with yours of order. Then together we can arrive at a design in which we both can see fulfillment from our separate perspectives."

(I beg my architect friends, chuckling at the distance between this talk and their memories of the Community Meeting from Hell, to remember that we are still operating in the idealized world of the conceptual framework. But remember too that without a framework through which to understand its dynamics, the meeting actually is merely hellish, incomprehensible. With a framework, we can understand how it's going wrong and what we might do to get it back on track.)

With reference to our design act of the cosmetics counter in the department store, the Community discourse, in the persons of the sales staff, might well have desires not only about how they serve customers but about how they communicate among themselves (especially as they cope with times of customer overload) and how they might be able to take periodic short respites from customers when demand is slack.

All of these desires about inhabitation (for that is what they truly are) could be communicated to the architect, not in terms of desired formal configurations (that would be doing the architect's work for her) but in terms of the *here-there* sense that would make each condition comfortable for them, and thus in conformance with their values.

With that as a charge, the architect would have a range of options from which to choose those design acts that all the discourses—Market, Community, *and* Design—could imagine would lead to their particular conceptions of fulfillment.

Again, this is an idealized situation. The maintenance staff doubtless would have other desires about clearances around the sales counters for its floor washers. But with good will, it is possible that there can be achieved a consensus vision of the shared life of all of the department store staffs. And whatever the outcome, I would have more faith in that rough consensus than in a consensus forged among the management with its Market values or by the architect with her Design values. Better to work from a difficult but authentic whole than from one that is easier but potentially false.

The next chapter will show the difficulty of achieving that authentic whole but will also suggest some of the design-act possibilities that come out of squarely facing the challenge.

5

Talking across Ways of Thinking

There is a phrase that has been lurking around the edges of our discussion about concord between values and surroundings. That phrase is *a sense of place.* I've been avoiding the term because it is so loaded with meanings that are not precisely what I want to convey by "concord." Most people who use the phrase would say that our inhabitants of the Missoula region feel a sense of place, but fewer would call what I felt at the Eames house "place," and almost no one would apply the phrase to a cosmetics sales counter no matter how closely it was attuned to the staff's desires. I, though, want to be able to see all three of these situations as instances of the same phenomenon, a setting in concord with its inhabitants' values about how to live.

Yet the term "place" has such resonance that I hesitate to give it up. Using the term would also open up connections with a large literature in which writers both describe locales and share with us the feelings those places engender in them and in others. In such writings we can feel the concord between setting and values vividly, right on the page.

So if with all my words I have established in your mind the category "concordance of surroundings and values," then let us agree that we can call that condition, additionally, "a sense of place."

It's in fact because of its vividness that I've chosen to examine place feeling through literature rather than through architecture. Plus, remember that we are concerned here not just with understanding how people feel about places but with seeing those individual feelings resolved into a whole vision of inhabitation—and resolved in a way that is authentic, a true reflection of the inhabitants' values about living. In a work of architecture, no matter how closely attuned to its inhabitants, that resolution of individual feelings will inevitably be bent in the direction of Design values, probably the more so if the work is esteemed by criticism. With a work of literature there will be less likelihood of such distortion.

So what I sought in my researches was a book that described and reflected upon a variety of places in a locale and then reconciled those reflections into a vision of living there. I found such a book, and such a locale, in *Old Jules* by Mari Sandoz.[1]

It is certainly not a book well known today (although it was highly praised at the time of its publication), and the places it describes will be unfamiliar to most readers. But it is because you will thus have few already fixed ideas about the places described that the book is so suited to the experiment I want to conduct.

Ostensibly a biography of her father, *Old Jules* is more truly a story about life in the days of settlement in the Sand Hills country of northwestern Nebraska. In it Mari Sandoz talks about places in a whole range of sizes, from the Sand Hills themselves to the Sandoz farmsteads and on down to their farmhouses and places within them. What I want to do is recount to you Sandoz's presentation of several such places, her description of each and the emotions it engendered, so you can feel with her the concord between place and feeling.

Then, for each place, will come the experiment. I will propose to you a particular *here-there* sense as the basis for her place feeling. And then will come the real leap: I will suggest design acts that can engender a similar *here-there* sense.

The purpose of the experiment is twofold. First, highlighting the *here-there* sense, describing it and giving it a name, helps us think of the feeling apart from its engendering place. Thinking of the feeling in this abstracted way, we can compare it to the place and so become aware of the ways in which it is a feeling appropriate to the emotions and values people hold about the place. This link-up of feeling and place is important to us because we have been looking for a way in which the Community orientation could translate its feelings and values into a charge to the architect. A vocabulary of *here-there* senses could be a vehicle for interrogating those values: the architect could ask, "If the sales counter had this *here-there* sense about it, would that sense seem appropriate to you, in concord with your feelings?"

But identifying an appropriate *here-there* sense and formulating it as a charge to the architect is of no help unless the architect can meet that charge by matching that sense with proposals for design acts. The second part of the experiment tries to show how design acts familiar to architects can be rethought in terms of the *here-there* senses they can engender, thus rendering them connectable to the kinds of concerns voiced in the Community discourse.

I hope this "How should it feel?" talk, like the conversation I imagined having just now with the sales staff, sounds familiar to my fellow architects. "How should it feel?" is one of the questions we frequently pose to our clients about a particular space, in our attempts to tease out some directives for our designing. I hope that after reading their way through this chapter, my colleagues will agree that truly all I am proposing here is a way of systematizing that familiar process and seating it in a larger conceptual framework.

I also hope that all my readers, not just the architects, will enjoy these incidents from *Old Jules* that I'm about to present. A demonstration of place feeling could have been conducted in far fewer pages than I am about to expend, but that shortened compass could not have conveyed Mari Sandoz's presentation of the sere Sand Hills emotional life that gives each of the places its resonance. You would also have missed a good story.

But before I can start the story of *Old Jules,* I need to acquaint you with its setting.

The Nebraska Sand Hills

Carey McWilliams coined the term "an island on the land" for Southern California, but the phrase conveys precisely the feeling of the Nebraska Sand Hills. The Sand Hills are easily described, geographically. They are grass-covered sand dunes forming an almond-shaped area roughly 130 miles by 260 miles in extent, wedged into the borders of Nebraska as it narrows to its "panhandle" in the northwest. But that cryptic description conveys little of the feeling they engender, little of their powerful sense of place.

Nebraska Sand Hills

Approaching them, especially from the southeast, you can see the Sand Hills rising out of the flatter Plains, with an abruptness that makes you imagine that you could plant your foot at the base of the first of them and say, "Here the Sand Hills begin."

It's an impression aided, no doubt, by highway speed, but with that same speed you are quickly past the first dunes and into the Hills' midst. And for the first time in perhaps a thousand miles on your westward journey, your horizon is not the far curve of the earth but the near crest of a range of mounded grassy hills, a hundred and more feet high. You feel enveloped, enfolded. You know that in places like Vermont there are hill-and-valley landscapes that are topographically similar. But because you know that beyond these hills are the boundless flat Plains, the spatial feeling of these hills is altogether different. It is an emphatic sense of *insideness.*

The wind contributes to that sense of being inside. It's a little gentler here than "outside" on the Plains. You imagine almost that the Plains winds are *up there,* high over your head, grazing the tops of the hills in their great continental sweep.

And then there are the hills themselves, which are softly rounded and rise up out of flat valley-bottoms with a plant-your-foot abruptness that is, this time, not imagined but almost actual. They are covered in grass, but not densely as in the East. It's a continuous cover, but sparse, in the Western mode—not hills of grass but hills with grass growing on them. And as is the pattern in the West, the grass is a mixture of colors never seen in the East—tans, blues, mauves, and sage greens—that vary with the light and with the seasons.

These are of course the rhapsodic maunderings of a visitor who doesn't have to wrest a living out of this place. For a long time in the nineteenth century, settlers could imagine no way at all of subsisting in the Sand Hills. Both farmers and ranchers saw the Hills as a desert waste. Clearly to them the Sand Hills were a place, but a useless place. Clearly too they felt a *here-there* sense about the Hills, but not a sense felt from being within them. It was more nearly a sense they felt emanating from the Hills, a sense they read as "Keep Out."

That conception changed though, and quite by accident. A highway historical marker on Route 20, on the northern edge of the Sand Hills, today tells the story of cattlemen who, in the 1870s, kept their herds out of the Hills, convinced that cattle could not survive there. Then one day, several head of cattle wandered away from a herd and into the Sand Hills. The cattlemen had given them up for lost until, quite some time later and almost as a whim, they decided to go and seek them out. To quote the sign, "They entered the Sand Hills" and found the cattle thriving. The cattle had found not only plenty of grass to eat but, most significantly, a number of small ponds to drink from.

Instantly the cattlemen's conception of the Sand Hills was transformed. They now saw the place not as a desert to avoid but as a cattle-feeding ground to exploit. Acting on their new beliefs, they conspired to lock up this wasteland-turned-precious-resource for themselves. And, in conformance to long-standing Western tradition, they got Congress to declare the Sand Hill counties closed to claims by homesteaders, a prohibition they would keep in force until the early years of the twentieth century.

That phrase on the highway marker—"They entered the Sand Hills"—tells us much about the *here-there* sense the Hills engender. It tells us of the feeling of a *border,* on one side of which is *here,* and on the other, the absence or complement of *here*—that is, *there.*

Certainly the cattlemen at first felt that. For them, *here* was the flat land around the Hills where cattle could graze. Inside the border of the Hills was to them a kind of void. A *border* feeling both grew out of and accorded with their values about the Hills.

I, in contrast, was not avoiding the Hills but seeking them out, so I came upon them with the opposite valuation. For me the Hills were the positive entity, the land around was the void. A *border* sense of *here-there* matched my orientation, but from the opposite direction. For me, the Hills were the *here,* the surrounding terrain the *there,* that "plant your foot" edge the border between the two.

A *border* feeling likely expresses how the homesteaders felt about the Hills, but a little more complexly. We can imagine their minds flickering between two orientations, depending on what they were most attending to at any given moment. When in the grips of the feeling that "the grass is greener on the other side," they likely saw the locked-up Hills as the positive entity, the *here,* a glittering prize denied to them. When in a "let it be" mood, they probably saw their own flat lands as the positive *here,* the Sand Hills as that place "not for us."

Places with a *bordered* sense of *here-there* can often have about them this quality of alternating complementarity. Think of the *campo* of Siena, or any courtyard carved out of the solid stuff of a building— a cloister, say. Enter the *campo* along one of its passageways from the dense city, or look down on it from an upper window, and it does indeed have the feel of a great void cut out from the *here* of the city fabric. But when the famous *palio* horse race fills it, the *campo* becomes unquestionably the charged entity, the *here;* the city surrounding it is merely the thing that is "looking on." Similarly for a courtyard: is the space of the court the precious *here* or is it the *there* we look onto from our *here* surrounding it? The answer depends upon what you are attending to, what value you are attaching to one place or the other.

A *bordered* sense can thus give a feeling of concord to two different value structures, each feeling it possesses the charged half of the *here-there* complement, the good fences between making good neighbors (as long as neither feels resentment with his lot). But what remains, as the valuations flicker back and forth, is the border that each feels to exist between them.

The border thrown around the Sand Hills by the cattlemen rankled many homesteaders, but none so significantly, for our exploration of place, as Old Jules Sandoz.

"Old Jules Country"

Who, you are entitled to ask, is Old Jules Sandoz? The objective answer is simple enough. He was a Swiss immigrant who settled in the Sand Hills region in 1884, and the subject of the biography *Old Jules* written by his daughter Mari Sandoz and published in 1935. You could go a little deeper and say that he was a leading figure in the settlement of the region, helping to establish many other immigrants on neighboring farms. And you could say that he was a pioneering horticulturalist, introducing many plant species into the region and showing how they could be grown there. But none of that conveys what Old Jules Sandoz *means*.

What *Huckleberry Finn* is to the middle Mississippi, what *Ramona* was to Southern California, what *Gone with the Wind* once was to Atlanta—that is what *Old Jules* is to Nebraska and especially the Nebraska Panhandle. This is the book that showed the region a picture of itself so compelling that ever after, any sense of the place would be conditioned by the images it laid down in popular memory.

What compels about *Old Jules* is not just that its title character is so interesting and characteristic (irascible, opinionated, tough-as-nails) but that his story recapitulates the whole founding era of the region—from the precarious sod-house existence of the 1880s, through the drought times and the boom times at the turn of the century, to the moment in the 1920s when a tentative ease seemed finally to descend upon the land. Nebraskans can put the book into the hands of their children (as they do through their school systems[2]) and say to them, "That is how we got to be what we are. That is how this place got to be what it is."

Nowhere is this book-engendered sense of place more pervasive than in "Old Jules Country," the northwest edge of the Sand Hills, the region where on the map the Panhandle of Nebraska attaches to the bulk of the state. Visit there and you will drive with the aid of county maps dotted with sites mentioned in the book, and an "Old Jules Trail" highlighted for you. Alongside the roads you will find historical markers commemorating Mari Sandoz and her father, hand-lettered signs directing you to her grave, even a marble slab (incised with the portrait of Old Jules from the book's frontispiece) marking the "Site of Well Accident *Old Jules* page 100." At the back of a crafts store in one of the towns is a museumlike Mari Sandoz Room, with mementos in glass cases and clippings in scrapbooks. In almost any drugstore you will find new editions of Mari Sandoz's books, difficult to find in even the largest bookstores in Lincoln or Omaha.[3]

Not only does your memory of the book condition how you see and feel the place, the book itself pervades the place, seems almost present there. So here is another *here-there* sense engendered by the valuation one puts on a place. Coming into the region with *Old Jules* on my mind, I felt a kind of *here* wherever I went, and not only when encountering places from the book. When you "know" a region from a book (especially if you don't know too much about it *besides* what you have read in books), you find that the stories can "explain" everything you encounter—people's habits and accents, the shape of their houses and the land. All of the region becomes for you a single *here* through the agency of the book. You feel as if some emanation of the book had pervaded the region, seeping into everything and uniting it like a benign, invisible fog.

Call this sense of *here*-ness *pervasive*. It inheres not in the form of something, nor even in how we use it or inhabit it, but in what we *think* about it. Anytime publicity of any kind—television, movies, literature, folk tales—precedes our experience of a place, we see everything about the place, to some extent, through that lens of "what we know about it." Diverse and unfocused as it might be to people unconditioned by the publicity, to us who "know" it in that way, it is a single *here*.

How Jules got his land

Of all the literary personalities that exemplify place, Old Jules Sandoz is perhaps the most unlikely—and unlikeable. As painted by his daughter, he is a seething bundle of resentments: he drives away two wives, keeps one only by trickery, manhandles his children, feuds with his neighbors and with the government.[4] In choosing the site for his farm, he seemed determined to pick the very place that would most confirm him in his sense of persecution, the high flat lands just across the Niobrara River, from which the forbidden Sand Hills would be daily seen. (The river's name is pronounced "nye-*brair*-uh.") Important to us though, for this study of place, is how Old Jules envisioned not just his farm's relationship to the Sand Hills but the farm itself as an entity.

Jules was settling his farm under the provisions of the Homestead Act of 1863. As is well known, that act allowed a person to stake a claim to 160 acres of public land and—after occupying the land for a certain amount of time, adding certain improvements and paying certain fees—to assume ownership. Those requirements for ownership changed continually throughout the settlement period, but the method of claim continued unchanged.[5] The hoped-for model, not always followed, was this:

In advance of settlement the land would have been surveyed into one-mile square *sections*, each containing 640 acres. The federal surveyors would mark the corners of the sections by digging "four holes, one in each of the cornering sections, the soil thrown together into a central mound, and a stake bearing the section numbers driven into the mound."[6] The 160 acres allotted for homesteads were thus achieved by dividing the 640-acre section along its center lines, north-south and east-west, into quarter-sections. (Surveying these "interior lines" was the responsibility of the homesteaders, a job often done by "locators," subject to later verification by government surveyors.)

Thus when you, a homesteader in virgin territory, found a site that seemed propitious, your first task was to find the nearest surveyors' stake and from its markings determine which quarter-section your potential farm fell into. Prudence would then dictate a quick reconnoitering of your quarter-section, roughly pacing off its boundaries with a hand-compass to see what fell within them—or outside of them: sighting a spring on the "wrong" side of your boundary might prompt you to pick that quarter-section instead, in which case you'd have to repeat the process. Once you were satisfied with your choice and had noted, from the stake at one of its corners, its section number and quadrant within the section, you would ride to the local land office, where the officials would pull out the surveyors' maps, locate your quarter-section on them, and, if no one had staked a prior claim, record you on the map as the designated homesteader of those 160 acres.[7]

The lands just west of the Sand Hills had been surveyed in 1881 and thus were opened to settlement.[8] An incident from *Old Jules* shows both the operation of this section system and the way that it could give Jules a peculiar sense of groundedness, of *here*-ness, in a landscape not yet known and thus undifferentiated to him.

Old Jules finds the survey stake

Jules had just pitched a tent on his intended claim but hadn't yet scouted his land or sought out the corner stake when

a man, his wife, and a daughter of eighteen shivered through a three-day drizzle at Jules's camp. They laughed at the settler's pan-fried bread and his coffee pounded with a hammer in the corner of a flour sack. But they listened eagerly enough when he talked of preemptions and timber claims and read the Homestead Act to them . . . [9]

Over the course of the three days, Jules convinced himself that his rough wooing had won him the heart of the daughter. But the next morning he arose to find the ground dusted in snow, his visitors gone (and with them his hopes for a wife), and worse, his horses wandered off. Immediately he set out to find them. Then:

At the edge of a bluff he stumbled over a stake, a corner stake, blurred, but with the numbers still discernible. The horses forgotten, he freed the needle of his pocket compass and stepped off the line towards his camp, each step one yard, north and east . . . Only when he had the numbers of his claim did the homeseeker look up. It was noon; the snow was gone, and bobolinks rose from the prairie, spiraling into the air until they were only specks against the light sky, raining melody as they coasted to the earth. Cap pushed back, Jules listened and sang a song of his student days in Zurich.

Once more everything was good.[10]

Clearly this is a way of envisioning land not seen anywhere on earth before the institution of the Rectangular Survey in the United States. Once land is seen in this way, as interchangeable squares of acreage, our whole orientation to land-as-place changes. I know of no instance where this new orientation is made more vivid than in Jane Smiley's recent novel *A Thousand Acres,* in which two families are destroyed by their desire for the same piece of land. In former times, such covetousness might have been centered on a precious spring or river frontage—some natural feature that distinguished one piece of land from another. Here the desire is for *acreage* pure and simple, and abstract. The book opens with these words, a farm woman speaking a memory from her childhood:

At sixty miles per hour, you could pass our farm in a minute, on County Road 686, which ran due north to the T intersection at Cabot Street Road . . .

Because the intersection was on this tiny rise, you could see our buildings, a mile distant, at the southern edge of the farm. A mile to the east, you could see three silos that marked the northeastern corner, and if you raked your gaze from the silos to the house and barn, then back again, you would take in the immensity of the piece of land my father owned, six hundred forty acres, a whole section, paid for, no encumbrances, as flat and fertile, black, friable, and exposed as any piece of land on the face of the earth . . .

If you looked west from the intersection, you saw . . . two sets of farm buildings surrounded by fields. In the nearer set lived the Ericsons . . . and in the farther set lived the Clarks . . . Harold Clark was my father's best friend. He had five hundred acres and no mortgage. The Ericsons had three hundred seventy acres and a mortgage.

Acreage and financing were facts as basic as name and gender in Zebulon County. Harold Clark and my father used to argue at our kitchen table about who should get the Ericson land when they finally lost their mortgage . . . I recognized the justice of Harold Clark's opinion that the Ericson land was on his side of the road, but even so, I thought it should be us . . . I thought it appropriate and desirable that the great circle of the flat earth spreading out from the T intersection of County Road 686 and Cabot Street Road be ours. A thousand acres. It was that simple.[11]

In finding the survey stake, Jules knew that he had found his *here,* his quarter-section of land. Jane Smiley tells us what Jules would come to know, how land *feels* under this system—continuous, articulated, and interchangeable.

What is perhaps surprising is that Jules, raised in a Swiss tradition of ancestral land tenure and place-by-natural-features, would so quickly shed his native conceptions and adopt wholesale this new, abstract cognition of place on the land. In *Old Jules* we see him shifting his land holdings several times—to get better land or to avoid neighbors for whom he had conceived a dislike, even exploiting a loophole in the Homestead Act that allowed a wife to claim her own quarter-section (resulting, with his last wife, in a claim of two plots of land that were noncontiguous).

This is a sense of *here-there* that is divorced from human sensory experience. Unless your land happens, like that of Jane Smiley's narrator, to have a rise, you cannot actually see your farm. You can know its extent only through the abstraction of a map.

And when you consult that map (either in fact or in memory), you realize that the extent of your farm—its shape, its borders—has no "necessity," no inherent reason (a natural feature, say) for being the way it is. No set of nature-given features defines the borders of your farm: your farm and all the farms that touch it counterdefine each other. It's almost impossible to imagine "my farm" without in the very same thought imagining the farms that surround and define it.

It's a situation very much like the one presented to us by the yin-yang symbol: to imagine the yin half is to imagine the yang half, so counterdefining, so interlocked are they. *Interlocked* is in fact a name we can give to this particular *here-there* sense. And its best analogue in design comes perhaps in the work of Carlo Scarpa. Scarpa's whole career was an effort to interlock solid with void, material with material, space with space. To imagine any space, any *here*, in a Scarpa design is to imagine its counterdefining, complementary *there*. It goes without saying that spaces in the work of Scarpa's progenitor Frank Lloyd Wright have the same *here-there* sense of being *interlocked* with each other. And both have acknowledged their debt to Japanese examples like the Katsura Imperial Palace and its gardens.

But a slight turn of the mind, a different valuation, can make us feel about this gridded landscape a different *here-there* sense, one akin to that *pervasive* feeling we saw a moment ago. And we feel it for the same reason, because of "something we know"—in this case the Rectangular Survey system.

The map that is our vehicle for knowing the extent of our *here* also tells us of the almost infinite mile-square grid in which our *here* is located. Tweak the mind only a little bit and it's possible to imagine that grid pervading the region, the state, the nation, obliterating boundaries, making to our perception one huge *here*.

Equally pervasive is a grid of columns, especially as Le Corbusier taught us to see it. His now-common insight was to have us see a column-grid not merely as a rational way to hold buildings up but as a way to imagine them. He invited us to think of a terrain as covered and controlled by an unbroken grid of potential columns, the building then being only a materialization of some of the columns, the rest still present in the imagination, pervading our sense of the building and its surroundings.

Today we not only design buildings on this basis but are accustomed to seeing them in this way, especially when the regularity and extent of the column-grid is presented to our experience with sufficient force. By extension, architects know that any regularized system (parallel party walls, a pervasive geometry, etc.), if presented forcefully enough, can engender in our minds the sense that a kind of *here* pervades every place the system pervades.

Old Jules builds his first house

Old Jules's first dwelling was a pretty makeshift affair, erected as much to establish his homestead claim as to provide shelter. "Between hunts and helping settlers find corners and lines, Jules worked at his dugout, two thirds in the ground, roofed with sod over straight ash poles."[12] Weeks later, the hut was still without a wooden floor or door,[13] but it had yet become something of a social center for the area ("There was always news at Jules's dugout, companionship, good talk. Often, too, there was a glass of wine, pieplant at first, currant later in the summer."[14]), and it even housed the local post office ("With black grease from the wagon axle and a corn cob he painted the words POST OFFICE in eight-inch letters. This he nailed over his door, a foot and a half above the ground of Mirage Flats."[15]). Of all of this Jules was inordinately proud: for him the dugout was a place of companionship and an emblem of his importance in the community.

We can imagine what kind of *here-there* sense this dugout had for Jules and his fellows, especially as the home-made wine flowed and darkness fell. Sitting there in the lamplight, the companions probably became aware of only *this place here,* their consciousness of the surrounding country and all its hardships obliterated in the face of the conviviality inside.

There are certainly places in architecture that engender in us the feeling that "this is all there is." We get such a feeling when we stand in the Pantheon, and by extension, any work that seems so complete that we can't imagine anyplace else—the Tempietto of Bramante, for example, or Thomas Jefferson's demi-Pantheon, the University of Virginia Rotunda.

But it doesn't require roundness to engender what we might call an *isolated here-there* sense. The inside of a theater always gives us that feeling, and so usually does the inside of a church.

In all these cases an *isolated* feeling accords with the desire to think, or believe, that *this place here* is all that matters right now.

Henriette builds Jules's second house

When it came time to bring his mail-order bride from Neuchâtel home from the train, Jules saw his dugout for how it actually appeared.

Jules did not take Henriette to his dugout immediately. After considering a photograph of this woman with lace at her wrists, he decided it should not be so, at first . . . For the present he made arrangements to use the Rutter shack, near the river, and all above ground.

It was dark when Jules and his bride arrived . . . When it was time for bed she roused herself and slowly, with uncertain movements, she spread new linens from her trunk over the blankets she suspected were dirty if she could see them clearly. Once she stopped and looked about as if one just awakening. It could not be true—this . . . [16]

Towards morning it began to rain. The roof leaked, a little at first, then more. Soon everywhere. Henriette sat on the wet straw tick all the next day with a purple umbrella over her head, crying noiselessly while Jules raged that there was no fuel.

Henriette kept her silence, recognizing that she was stuck in this strange new land. But when Old Jules got her to file a homestead claim in her own name, she laid her plans.

With his wife's money Jules wanted to build, like the peasants he saw in France, a grainery, a horse stable, a chicken coop, and a pigpen, in a succession of lean-tos against the living quarters. Henriette waited until he was away on a hunt. Then she hired two men to build a story-and-a-half house, and laid out a yard with outbuildings . . .

. . . Jules complained bitterly among the neighbors, but as soon as the roof was on he moved his guns, his [medicines], and his new stamp collection to his wife's place. Without a regret he left his dugout on Mirage flats forever.[17]

Gruff as the life of the Plains might have made him, Jules had nevertheless been born into the comfortable life of the Swiss bourgeoisie. For all that he might resent its provenance, this house offered itself as a place of remembered comfort, and he took it.

With Henriette's house now a *here* to him, what sense might Jules have had of the *there* of his abandoned dugout? If asked to think about it, he might have gestured in its general direction with words like, "It's out there somewhere, but I don't think about it much."

What he would be saying is that he feels no discernable relationship between *here* and *there*. *There* is merely "out there somewhere," *only-adjacent* to *here*.

If you have ever inhabited one of Frank Gehry's "each-room-a-building" compositions, you might have experienced something like an *only-adjacent* sense there. Each of the room-buildings feels so complete that when you are in any one of them, you almost have an *isolated*, "this is all there is" feeling. But something will have tipped you off to the presence of other places (a view through a window, a door leading from one room to another, that view you got of the whole complex . . .). You're aware of those other places, but because you can't quite pin down how they relate to the place you're in now, they only hover in your consciousness; they feel *only-adjacent*.

As we walk through the remains of Hadrian's Villa, we can imagine that the Roman emperor's guests might have felt something similar. When standing in any one of the villa's pleasure pavilions, it's almost impossible to imagine the way in which it relates to any of the other pavilions. The result is not just that your attention is focused almost exclusively on the place you're in. When you emerge into a different place, you can't for the life of you retrace how you got there. And so the new place comes as a complete and pleasant surprise—which is no doubt exactly the feeling Hadrian wanted his imperial guests to have.

The same effect happens to us in Disneyland, and out of the same motive. It comes as a shock to look at a guide-map and realize that all of the diverse attractions are actually cheek-by-jowl. But the relationships between them have been so disguised that we're left, when in each place, with the feeling that those other places are "somewhere else," *only-adjacent* to the place we are in now.

Exhibition design gives us another example of places specifically designed to hide from us any sense of where we are. Just try and draw a mental map of any multimedia exhibition space you have ever walked through. The intention in such exhibitions is obviously that the only space we feel is the "space" of information, which we imagine ourselves floating through.

In all these cases an *only-adjacent* sense of *here-there* accords with our desires for how to inhabit the place: for reasons of privacy or pleasure or information, we *want* to be only dimly aware of the presence of places other than the *here* we are experiencing.

Jules builds a house for Emilia; no: for *Mary*

Jules's pleasure in his new house didn't last long. Soon he was engaged in the bitterest of his land feuds, during which Henriette found herself being shot at by Jules's rivals. The case was settled against him in court, but

Jules, aggressive in his justification, fought the battles over and over. His neighbors could walk away from him, but not his wife. She heard it late into the night. And in the morning while her husband snored she pounded the stove lids and banged the water bucket until he awoke and cursed her from the bed. Finally at ten one morning she emptied the wash basin upon his head and then, her hair flying gray strings in the wind, drove her cart towards town. From the doorway, his ragged underwear dripping, he called her foul names. Standing up in her cart she hurled her challenge in his face, defying the rifle in his hand.[18]

When the divorce was finalized, Jules found himself not only without a wife but without a house and farm (it was *her* quarter-section, remember). Buying up the mortgage of his former rival in the land feud, he had a new farm and, at least as important, a final victory in his claim wars. And learning (for once) from his experience, he thought he knew what kind of house it would take to impress, and keep, a new wife. Like an architect designing for an imagined client, he would bring *that* place into existence.

He built the best house he ever possessed—two rooms with an attic and a cellar. He sent for a good maple bedroom set, with a fine big glass and good springs. With his name in eight-inch letters on a board over the door, there was nothing to do but wait.[19]

The enticement didn't work for Emelia, the next in his string of mail-order Swiss brides, but it was enough to convince another emigrée, Mary. She stayed, her staying a mixture of resignation to him and the anticipation of possibilities for herself. It was into that house that Mari and her brothers and sisters were born—a house whose genesis was thus a mixture of spite, calculated enticement, and unadmitted imagery of bourgeois comfort and ease. So what the house *embodied* to its inhabitants was a combination of all that, to which were added the qualities that Mary and the children brought to it out of the experiences they lived there.

Those experiences conditioned how each of the family members imagined the house, and how each of them saw the various *parts* of the house.

Mary whitewashes the bedroom

Take the bedroom, the half of the house that Jules and Mary shared, which Jules had furnished with the expensive bedstead as an enticement to prospective brides and as proof to himself of his prosperity. The room doubtless spoke other things to Mary. But then one summer came the prospect of fancy visitors from Switzerland, who would of course have the room to themselves for the duration of their visit.

Late in June Mary was whitewashing the bedroom, her face and clothing splattered . . . She scrubbed up the white patches on the floor and was pleased that the kalsomine on the walls was drying much less streaked and much whiter than she had hoped.

With homemade lye soap she scoured the chairs . . . She dragged the lounge out and pounded it clean of dust, recalling that once there were even bugs in it . . . She looked at her bedroom, white as a hospital room, with the maple set Jules bought for Emilia. At least it had a good mirror.[20]

The bedroom was to be made to recall, to the visitors (and to Mary and perhaps Jules) the refinement of homes in Bern and Zurich. For Jules and Mary it must also have been an implicit invitation to live for a while not in their present reality but in the better reality sure to come here in the Plains. When the visitors returned to Switzerland, surely their remembered presence (and the remembered and possible world their visit had recalled) conditioned how Mary and Jules saw the room when they resumed possession of it.

We can certainly imagine that the room no longer felt like merely "that part of the house behind the plank partition." Likely the house came to feel, on some level, like two places, each a *here* to the other's *there.*

It was, though, a small and simple house. Much as you might feel one room to be a *here,* you would likely feel, almost as strongly, the near presence of the other room *there.* When in either of the rooms, you would likely characterize the other room with phrases like "the room next door," "the room on the other side of the wall." The *here-there* sense you would feel would be one of *relatedness.*

We spend much of our lives in rooms that feel *related* to other rooms. It doesn't go too far to say that a driving motivation of Western architecture from the Renaissance to the modern period was to *relate* rooms in clear, identifiable ways.

One way to make spaces feel *related* is to put them on-axis with each other. Or a space might be an alcove off of another, or overlooking another. The common hallmark of such spaces is that we characterize them less by what they are than by how they relate to someplace else. And as we characterize them, so do we often feel them—as a *here* related to a *there.* Each of these relationships says something different about the two spaces being related. A feeling of place can be said to happen when that "thing said" accords with how life is lived in them.

We saw in chapter 1 how an axial relationship can speak "equivalence." A strongly felt relationship can also, for example, speak "hierarchy." It's likely that Jules and Mary, both before and after the visitors, managed how the room they shared would relate to the rest of the house (through door closings, furniture placement, and house rules) so that the relationship would embody to all the Sandozes the valuation that the bedroom was "smaller but more special" than other spaces in the house.

Jules builds a lean-to onto the house

The very word "lean-to" speaks of a relationship, one of dependence on a larger thing. But geometry is not destiny. A geometrically related place can be imbued with a different *here-there* sense if that other sense will better accord with the inhabitants' image of how they wish to live.

One day Jules received a letter from Rosalie, the only real love of his life, and her new husband. Bourgeois, sophisticated Swiss, they were visiting New York and were contemplating a railroad trip to the Sand Hills of which Jules had written to her so glowingly.

On the strength of her message, and in his hopes of recapturing some of the thwarted promise of his youth, "Jules went to town the next day and with what remained of Mary's money bought lumber for a lean-to of two rooms on the north."[21]

But when a second letter arrived announcing their imminent return to Switzerland, Jules, ever stoic in the face of dashed hopes, moved his workshop into the lean-to. What thoughts he must have had there, as he worked over his blacksmith forge, of the life he might have had with Rosalie. What a poignant sense of place he must have felt there.

But life on the Plains made little allowance for might-have-beens. Mary's mother (who was now living with them) fell ill, the victim of old age and an infected cut on her forehead from one of Jules's orchard trees. As she declined, she was installed in the lean-to, turned from imagined bower of refinement to productive workshop to, now, a place of impending death.

The inevitable came, and after the burial, Jules was ever-stoic (or maybe just insensitive).

At home Jules threw open the grandmother's room to the November winds as soon as she was gone. Sucking at his pipe, he planned for another occupant. Governor Mickey had agreed to let him have a convict on parole."[22]

—for which he would be paid a stipend. The bower/workshop/sickroom now became merely a room for rent. But perhaps somewhere in Jules's mind was the thought that by the installation of this utter stranger he could convince himself that this place of thwarted memory, then work, then death, was not a part of the *here* of his home at all, even though *related,* as a lean-to, by both geometry and structure.

In our terms, he would have been trying bring himself to feel an *only-adjacent* sense about the lean-to: "It's back there somewhere; I don't much think about it." Jules could have brought about this feeling in himself by various means—by shutting up the door to the lean-to and cutting a new outside door, or merely by enforcing on the convict rules about his comings and goings, rendering the visitor invisible to his experience. (We can easily believe Jules imperious enough to ignore the convict's passages through the main house to the lean-to. Not for Jules was there any of Viollet's democracy-engendered unease!)

Marie reads in the attic

The house had one more part in addition to the two rooms on the ground floor, the half-story loft where Marie slept once she was big enough to climb the ladder. (Christened "Marie," Sandoz later took "Mari" as her nom de plume when she encountered a numerologist who convinced her that the shortened name was more propitious.[23]) We can imagine how this place must have felt spatially: the floorboards transparent to sound (and more blessedly, heat) from the rooms below, the near presence overhead of the flimsy rafters and their board sheathing.

But most times Marie was not attending to the fragile spatial shell covering her, but to the world she could inhabit through her books.

Although Jules disapproved of fiction of any kind for his family, she smuggled books in the baggy blouses she wore at that time and carried them up the outside ladder to bury in her lumpy straw mattress in the attic . . . No one would discover her there. Jules could not climb the ladder, so she could read undisturbed at night by lantern light.[24]

Here for her was a thing circumscribed by the light a kerosene lamp could throw upon the pages as she turned them. With her attention focused on the pages of her book, Marie likely felt that *isolated* sense of *here*-ness, aware of nothing else but the world contained within the circle of lamplight.

But all of us possess several senses of how we wish to live, and when we shift from one sense to another, we attend to different parts of the world around us. In so doing we can bring about a different, more concordant *here-there* sense. We can guess that when Marie heard voices coming up through the boards from the rooms below, then she might have felt a *bordered* sense of *here-there*. We can picture her abandoning her book, noiselessly getting on her hands and knees with one ear pressed against the border of the world below her.

Marie hides under the stove

Marie had learned her strategy of withdrawal into imagination early in life, before she was able to find escape in the black marks on a page.

When the little Marie was three months old and ill with summer complaint, her cries awakened Jules. Towering dark and bearded in the lamplight, he whipped the child until she lay blue and trembling as a terrorized small animal. When Mary dared she snatched the baby from him and carried her into the night and did not return until the bright day.

But the night's work was never to be undone. Always the little Marie hid away within herself.[25]

So when a family discussion turned heated, "Marie, who hung about the outskirts of all excitement, slipped into the dark nook behind the kitchen stove. There her mother found her the next morning."[26]

And even at Christmastime, when the gathered neighbors insisted that the children sing carols—

But the children could n't sing. [Her brother] Jule rumbled, Marie squeaked. When everybody laughed they cried and retreated, Jule to the grandmother, Marie behind the stove.[27]

Marie doesn't tell us anything about the space of her hiding place, but people on the Plains know that some turn-of-the-century stoves came with a water reservoir to one side of the oven, hanging down beneath the cooktop to about a foot-and-a-half off the floor. Perhaps it was there that Marie hid, invisible to others' sight but able to see and hear all that went on in the room (and kept pleasantly warm as well, the water in the reservoir retaining its heat between mealtime firings of the stove).

Marie in her hiding place reminds us that a *here-there* sense is not always reciprocal. It is possible to feel *related* to a *there,* as Marie surely does, without *there* feeling much of a relationship back. Places with this particular *here-there* sense can accord with deep longings in us—window seats, overlooks, windows from which we can look down. All of these can give us that sense of being an unseen observer, in a *here* tinier than, but commanding, *there.*

A hailstorm on the Plains

Let's turn back to the house as a whole, remembering that it is constructed of thin boards over a frame, and hear Marie's recounting of a Plains hailstorm.

By now the lightning was an almost continuous blinding violet; the thunder rocked the house.

Then suddenly the hail was upon them, a deafening pounding against the shingles and the side of the house, bouncing high from the ground in white sheets. One window after another crashed inward, the force of the wind . . . driving the hail in spurts across the floor, until white streaks reached clear across it. Water ran in streams through the wide cracks between the boards.

The wind turned, and the south windows, unprotected, crashed inward together, the house rocking with the blast.[28]

We can imagine that during these moments the Sandozes were hardly aware of the *parts* of their house, the two rooms and attic above. Their whole attention likely was focused, powerfully, upon the skin of the whole house, that skin their only protection against the hail. For them only two places were imaginable: *out there* in the storm and *in here* in the house, the two divided only by the border of resonating boards and shingles.

Let me characterize this particular *here-there* sense as a feeling of *continuity* within a *border:* you are more aware of the border between *here* and *there* than you are of the divisions within *here.*

There is an architectural parallel to this *here-there* sense, and it occurs, perhaps surprisingly, in Le Corbusier's Villa Savoie, specifically on the main floor. That floating rectangle of space certainly has a *bordered* sense about it, one world inside the border, a different world outside of it. But within the border, Le Corbusier has gone to great lengths to make the spaces feel *continuous* with each other, the spatial feeling of each of the main rooms flowing unbroken from indoors to out. This flow is accomplished by having the indoor and outdoor spaces *interlock* with each other in yin-yang fashion, the plan of the main floor being almost a squared-up yin-yang symbol. And just as was the case in earlier examples, the interlocking makes it difficult to be in one space without being aware of the other, complementary spaces that counterdefine the world you are aware of—in this case the mixed inside-and-outside world bounded by the rectangular walls. Your sense of *here* is constantly invited to expand its compass outward from the parts to the whole—and to see it, all of the whole within the border, as the real *here*.

Marie says good-bye to the river bottom

In 1904 the power of the cattle barons was broken, and the Sand Hills were at last opened to homesteading. The Sandoz family quickly staked a claim across the Niobrara and began constructing a new farmhouse. In the last days before the move, Marie would often steal away to a promontory near the old farmhouse. From there she could look down on the Niobrara river bottom that separated the hard land where she stood from the Sand Hills beyond. Standing there, she knew that in the new place, she

would never hear the thunder of the ice going out on the Niobrara again, never see the gold of autumn along the bluffs, the ash, slender yellow pencils, the cottonwoods rustling in chartreuse and orange, the creeper blood splashes on the silver of the buffalo berries.[29]

That river-bottom place can still be experienced by driving in a rental car along a sandy track to the county highway bridge that crosses the Niobrara a few yards downstream from the wooden pilings that mark the turn-of-the-century passage the Sandozes would have used to pass from the hard-land fringe to the Sand Hills themselves.

Through the windshield you can see the plant species described by the young Marie. Even in a car you feel the descent to the river bottom, and you realize that from down here the flat lands to the west are almost indistinguishable from the Hills to the east. All you can see from down here are bluffs on either side of the river bottom. But you know that up *there*, invisible but just beyond that eastern bluff, are the fabled Sand Hills.

The *here-there* sense of this place is surely one of being at a *border*. But I was reminded, there in Nebraska, of nothing so much as Alvar Aalto's library in Seinajoki, Finland. Standing in the fan-shaped bookstacks of that library, your attention is drawn up to the high louvered opening in the wall as it curves and recurves out of your field of vision, left and right. Its light, and the shape the louvers give to that light, promise the existence of another world *up out there* beyond the border, just as the bluffs here at the Niobrara river bottom promise you the existence of the Sand Hills beyond.

But then you open the door of your rental car to set foot on this place made special to you by literature, and you encounter the *flies* unmentioned by the progenitor of this place-feeling—*swarms* of them that invade your car (and will be with you for miles to come). They have been drawn here by the very things that made this river bottom such a place for a young girl at the turn of the century: abundant life fed by the waters, a refuge from the wind, a spatial enclosure made by land forms.

But once you accommodate yourself to the humming bites of the insects, you will experience something else Marie experienced, the rustling *hiss* of the cottonwoods, the trees whose leathery leaves turn the omnipresent winds of the Plains into a sibilant whisper.

Cottonwoods, you know from the trove of nature guides crowding your car's glove compartment, grow only along stream banks in this part of the Plains. And the same guidebooks tell you that streams almost always occur *beneath* the Plains, their waters having eroded the soft alluvial soil into minivalleys. But only in actual experience do you realize that these washes are populated not so much by the presence of these trees as by their sound. To descend into a streambed on the Plains is not so much to enter a space formed by earthen walls as it is to descend into a *sound*, inaudible above but inescapable below.

The phonograph comes to the Sand Hills

Marie felt the presence of another place made by sound in the new farmhouse in the Sand Hills, with the arrival of a mail-ordered phonograph.

When the father was home, the phonograph was kept going, even during his nap, as though to make up for all the miserable, musicless years. Marie's mother missed the family song hours. The supper dishes were no longer washed to old Swiss songs or to "My Old Kentucky Home" but probably to a facile piano solo, perhaps a fragment of a concerto that stopped Marie's hand in the dishwater, or perhaps to Ada Jones singing "If the Man in the Moon Were a Loon."[30]

We can imagine from our own experience how the music of the phonograph must have pervaded the whole house. But to imagine how that might have felt for the Sandozes, we have to subtract from our own mental image the sounds of cars whizzing by on the county road, and all the other sounds of modern life that we have been rendered, by familiarity, hardly conscious of. When we imagine the silence of the Plains in the 1920s, and insert into that silence the sheer novelty, then, of recorded sound, we realize that to hear a phonograph in such a setting must have been a truly attention-grabbing experience. The compass of its sound must indeed have felt like a single place, powering out of consciousness the merely spatial divisions of the house. And when summer came and the windows and doors would have been thrown open, the place of sound must have extended outdoors, making the farmyard and the house seem one *pervaded* place.

We can imagine as well that when the house was thrown open to the breezes in summer, the feel of the air itself, unchanged from indoors to out, must have made the place of the house feel *continuous* with the outdoors.

What the phonograph was to the Sandozes, television is to us today. And our experience with TV helps us imagine the different kind of place by sound the Sandozes likely felt when they would often go to a neighbor's house for a sing-along around that family's piano. As their voices rose, all their attention would have become focused on the source of the music, their directed attention almost obliterating their awareness of the space in which the sing-along was happening. A similar feeling likely was present in the Sandoz house when Jules played his violin or a visiting neighbor gave forth on the accordion.

In both cases, as the harmonies swelled and coalesced, everyone's attention would have become tightly focused in the direction of the music, everyone feeling *related* to the source of the music as a center. Those sitting outside the circle of singers might, if they thought about it, have felt themselves to be in a place concentric on the place made by the singers and the piano. They might well have been experiencing something akin to a *fan* of places centered on the piano, all their felt places set within (and for the moment lessening their awareness of) the other geometry of the walls of the house.

This instance not only tells us of another species of the *related* sense of *here-there*. It reminds us again that multiple senses of *here* can coexist, even simultaneously, in the same physical space. Depending upon what matters to us at any given moment, each of us will attend to different aspects of the world around us, and in each of our moments, imagine different *heres,* different *theres* out of a single surroundings.

Not only is this "the way people are;" it is for most of us vital that we be able freely to choose the compass and nature of the places we will most strongly identify with. For no one was that freedom more important than for Mari Sandoz.

A vision of life in the Sand Hills

For her, the writing of *Old Jules* was in many ways an exorcism, her attempt to break free of an identity as "daughter of the famous Jules Sandoz." Her task was complicated by the fact that the identity she felt as her own was tied up with the very place that defined *him,* the Sand Hills of Nebraska. *Old Jules* is thus an attempt to define a Sand Hills that are distinct from his and yet include his—a resolution of the different ways she and he and others felt about the place. Here are *those* Sand Hills:

To some of the settlers the sandhills seemed a soft, undemanding country, ideal for loafing. But only until the ranches extended no more credit on pancake flour, an invasion of sand fleas came, or the winds of winter swept down upon them out of the Dakotas. To others the country was aloof, austere, forbidding; the wind sucking their courage as it sucked the green from the grass by mid-June. Some saw it as a great sea caught and held forever in a spell, and were afraid. And here and there were a few sensitive to the constantly changing tans and mauves of the strange, rhythmical hills that crowded away into the hazy horizon. They heard the undying wind rattle the seed pods of the yuccas against the sky, sing its thin flute song over the tall, sparse grasses of the slopes. They smelled the strange odors of marsh and mint rising from the wet valleys at dusk, saw spring run in sudden fire of yellow blossoms over the low knolls and give way to deep blue. Then that too was gone as though no flower had ever been, until August brought the long, graceful white phlox blossoms and the reddening bunch grass turned to russet waves under the stern caress of the chill fall winds.[31]

6

The Good Life for an Architect

I'd like to look back at the last chapter and offer two observations, one merely interesting, the other central to the argument that will close this book. The interesting point comes if we rearrange the order of the *here-there* senses we uncovered. Reordered, the senses can form a kind of progression in which the compass of our awareness gradually increases.

With the sense that I called *isolated,* we are aware of only one place. With the *only-adjacent* sense, we are still primarily aware of only the place we're in, but we feel the presence, "out there somewhere," of something else. With the *related* sense, that something else comes into sharp focus: we are aware not just of the place we're in, we're aware of some other place and of a relationship between the two.

In the *bordered* sense, our compass of awareness grows. We imagine not just a few places but the proximate world, which we divide into two parts, *here* and "all the rest beyond the border." When *here* feels *pervaded,* our sense of "this part of the world" being one thing increases a notch.

With the *continuous* sense, our compass expands yet again. Over our sense of the proximate world as a divided thing we lay the idea of that world as a single continuous thing. With the *interlocked* sense, we actually experience the world as a single articulated thing, my *here* tightly counterdefined by other potential *heres.*

The progression thus doubles back on itself. From seeing *here* (this one place) as being all there is, we circle back around to see *here* (all these places) as all there is. An interesting thought but not, I hasten to add, "proof" of anything: we are having none of that in this book.

The second point, the one I want to develop, comes if we look not at the *here-there* senses themselves but at *what engendered those feelings.* What can make people feel the presence of a *here?*

A sense of *here* can be engendered through *shared memory* or *knowledge.*

• We saw, in my encounter with the highway historical marker, how a *historical moment* can make a place feel distinct. Certainly that's the motivation behind any country inn's claim that "George Washington Slept Here." More seriously, an ordinary stretch of boulevard in Dallas and an even more ordinary motel in Memphis have a sense of *here* for us because they were scenes of shocking, era-ending assassinations.

• *Literature* can imbue a region or a locale, or even a building, with a sense of *here,* as we saw with the regions made for us by Mari Sandoz and Mark Twain. In Salem, Massachusetts, Nathaniel Hawthorne's writings make the local House of Seven Gables, and even the desk he occupied at the Custom House, special places. Seeing a place in a movie can engender in us a shock of recognition, a *here* sense, when we later see that place in person. And as all of us in Boston well know, a beloved television series can make a neigborhood bar a nationally sought-out landmark.

• *Geographic, cartographic, or scientific knowledge* can make a place a *here.* My anticipation as I approached the Sand Hills, and my reaction to them, came largely out of what I had read about them in books on the geography of Nebraska. Old Jules's sense of his homestead claim and Jane Smiley's narrator's image of her farm came from their common map-knowledge of the Rectangular Survey. And the cattlemen's initial perception of the Sand Hills as a place to be avoided was based not on mere supposition but on a sciencelike (though incorrect) reading of the terrain.

A sense of *here* can be engendered through *shared practices*.

• Practices made common through *economics* can condition how we see a place. Certainly economics played a major part in Jane Smiley's narrator perceiving a thousand acres as a commodifiable entity. But economics (along with geography) also determines what farmers will plant, and once those planting practices become common, they can make people feel they inhabit a common place—"corn country" or "wine country," for example. Certainly this was a factor in the farmers and ranchers around Missoula feeling a common inhabitation.

• *Cultural practices* can shape how we feel about a place, whether it will be a *here* for us. It was cultural practices that impelled Mary to whitewash the bedroom, to give it at least one of the qualities of a fine Swiss room, to make it a *here*. And the house itself, and the lean-to behind it, had been shaped by Old Jules to match his own cultural preconceptions, so that each would qualify, in his eyes, as a *here*.

• And *here* can happen for us by *conventions of behavior*. My favorite example is that of two lovers in conversation: having eyes only for each other, and ears only for each other's words, they enact together a bubble of *isolated*, nothing-else-but-this, *here* around themselves, in total and blissful disregard for the shape of any space they might happen to be occupying. We can imagine that a *here* of that sort enwrapped Jules and Rosalie during their trysts in Switzerland. And a similar sense of isolation likely overtook Jules and his fellows during those nights in the dugout, the circle of their *here* becoming even smaller than the narrow compass of the dugout's earthen walls and boarded roof.

In our imagined scene at the ATM in colonial Virginia, cultural conventions would have erected a place of inviolability around the gentleman as he punched his access code into the apparatus. None of the surrounding yeomen would have dared breach that boundary all of them felt. And today a milder version of that inviolable *here* holds us in its grip when we stand behind someone transacting with the bank's machinery.

We can imagine that when the singing lapsed in the Sandozes' neighbors' house, the fan-shaped *heres* concentric on the piano would have collapsed in the minds of the singers, to be replaced by circles of conversation around topics of common interest. Probably, in that era, conventions of behavior would have dictated a circle of "man talk" and a circle of "woman talk," but each of those spherical *heres* would likely have existed without much reference to the walls of the space in which the conversations were conducted.

A sense of *here* can be engendered through *direct sensation*.

• During the hailstorm the Sandozes were acutely aware of the physical space they were in. They felt the walls of the house with that *spatial sense* that we know is a combination of our eyes seeing a space's extent, our ears hearing its sound, and our bodies sensing its temperature and its reverberance both from the air and from underfoot. Certainly Old Jules alone in his dugout felt something of that enclosing spatial sense, as did Marie when under the stove or up in her attic.

• We've seen how sensation itself can engender a sense of *here* that is apart from the space in which it occurs. We imagined that effect occurring when the outdoor air pervaded the Sandoz house in summer, and I felt it when the wind rustled the cottonwoods into sound at the river bottom.

We saw how sensation can be promulgated artificially to give us a sense of *here*. The sound of the phonograph pervading the house and making it a single place was an example of this *managed sensation*, as was the lamplight's demarcating a zone of *isolated* feeling for Marie from out of the larger attic.

• And finally, we saw one more instance where sensation made a *here* that was apart from spatial enclosure—when everyone's attention was focused on the piano in the neighbors' house. A moment ago we spoke about the conventions for using automatic teller machines, but our experience with ATMs is but another example, like that of the piano, of a *here* made for us by our *attention to apparatus*. In both cases, as we interacted with the apparatus, we partially lost our awareness of the physical space around us, replacing it with a smaller fan of *here* sense centered on the machine that for the moment had possession of our attention.

So there are a whole series of ways in which a sense of *here* can be engendered. There are thus also a series of ways to achieve that concord between values and feeling that we used the term *place* to name. For example:

Marie *wanted* to inhabit a secret world when she was reading in the attic: the lamplight engendered an *isolated* sense of *here* that matched her desires perfectly. You *want* to feel privacy when you transact business through an ATM: conventions of behavior engender the feeling of a *border* around you that achieves that private sense. Jules *wanted* to be able to exchange his farm for another if his circumstances changed: thinking in terms of the Rectangular Survey made him see the region as *continuous,* which made it possible for him to see each of his farms as exchangeable but also as a *here,* a home for him.

A sense of place was achieved in each case because a *here-there* sense appropriate to values was engendered—in these cases, through the agencies of managed sensation, conventions of behavior, and cartographic knowledge.

But when we remember that the achievement of place—values in concord with setting—constitutes partial fulfillment for the Community orientation, we might wonder if fulfillment for the Market could be achieved by similar means. Can the agents that engender a *here-there* sense for Community thinkers also *accomplish results* that can advance a marketing strategy? The answer, I want to persuade you, is that they can. Let's run through all the agents can can engender a *here* sense for Community thinking and see if those same agents can serve the Market discourse in its efforts to achieve its goal of marketplace substitution.

• The phrase "George Washington Slept Here" is not only a *here*-making piece of knowledge, it is also a venerable advertising slogan. Just as it conditions how a country inn feels to us, it also *positions* that inn among other inns, sets our expectations for it and, most crucially for what the Market hopes to accomplish, gives us a basis for choosing it over some competitor.

The analogue in the Market discourse for Community's *shared memory and knowledge* is, broadly speaking, *publicity*—that buzz generated by the marketers themselves, that put out by others, and that which is already known or believed by people in general. Advertisements, coverage in the media, word of mouth, our own prior experience or memory—all of these affect how we will see some offering in the marketplace. Any or all of these species of knowledge can play a part in accomplishing fulfillment for the Market discourse, getting its offering chosen over others.

• There are analogues in the Market discourse for *shared practices* as well. The pricing of a service or the rent structure of an office building or apartment are *economic practices* that will affect how we see the offering. *Cultural practices* will affect how we judge the offering, especially if, through publicity, those practices can be changed to the offering's advantage. Those of us of a certain age can well remember an American culture that didn't see "gourmet dining" as a practice ordinary people engaged in, and that had no concept at all of a "health club."

Conventions of behavior are changed when cultural practices change, and that too will affect how we imagine using or inhabiting a Market offering. But more directly under the Market's control are the behavioral conventions followed within a setting offered to our choice— the manner of intake at a clinic, the waiters' self-presentation in a restaurant, the governance, management, and programming of activities in a housing complex. Conventions like these have a truly determining effect on how users and inhabitants experience a place, and so are an equally determining factor in customers' and tenants' choices of a facility to patronize. A thorough marketing strategy today will have, as one of its component parts, the conventions of behavior that are to be promulgated in the setting the Market discourse offers.

• We have lots of experience with a marketing strategy using *direct sensation* as one of its components. The sound systems and choice of music in a high-fashion boutique is at least as important in determining its "feel" as the decor. Ambient sound is so common a factor in marketing that in some commercial environments we feel a real lack if there's no music in the air. And if when we are shopping a compelling sound mix unexpectedly cuts out, the character of the place changes utterly for us, almost as dramatically as if the lights had suddenly gone out.

Lighting is of course another *managed sensation* that often plays a part in marketing strategies. Like ambient sound, controlled lighting has become so ubiquitous in commercial environments that we notice it only when it is missing.

And don't overlook managed *smell* as a marketing ploy. Harvard Square has a famous hamburger joint that, for decades, has drawn customers by exhausting the enticing smells of its grill directly out onto the sidewalk over the heads of passing pedestrians. The sweeter analogue is the cinnamon-bun shop at the mall: they could exhaust their ovens to the outer air, but they're no fools!

As for the last two direct-sensation engenderers of here-sense, *space* and *attention to apparatus,* I need not detail for you the many, many ways the Market can use them as parts of its strategy to achieve substitution.

If all of this argumentation seems reasonable, let me draw from it a conclusion that might at first seem less than reasonable. That done, let me then answer some questions that the conclusion raises. We have said that the ideal of the building project is *fulfillment for all three discourses*—at the conclusion of the design, the reasonable expectation of fulfillment; with the habitation of the building, the achievement of fulfillment.

We saw further that it is *design acts* that bring about fulfillment. The way this happens is that the discourses look at a design act, and from their perspective, see in it the possibility of achieving a part or all of what they think the building is for.

This scheme still leaves undefined what a design act *is,* though. Conventionally we architects have defined our design actions as the shaping of space, with perhaps a few ventures into the design of sensation, most usually in the form of lighting. What this chapter has shown thus far is that fulfillment for the discourses we work with can be achieved by a much larger range of tools than that. If we were to follow this analysis of "what achieves fulfillment" out to its logical conclusion, we might conclude that a design act could be seen as *any shaping by the architect of knowledge, practices, or sensation.*

There's a proposition implicit in this conclusion, and for the purposes of argumentation, let me state the proposition baldly, in a concrete instance, so as to throw it into high relief for your consideration. Suppose we as architects were commissioned to design a restaurant. Working under this theory, we would see it as our charge to use design acts to fulfill our own "inclusion in narratives" goal, the "positioning within the marketplace" goals of the owners, and the "values about dining" goals of the interested community (which would comprise the patrons, the staff, local civic groups, and the government). Seeing the job that way, we might find ourselves asking to have a hand in designing not just the form and decor of the restaurant, not just its lighting, but its sound mix, its menus, and its graphics. We might ask for a say in the design of the uniforms of the wait-staff and their manner of addressing the patrons, and in the publicity for the restaurant (vital not just in marketing but in setting the Community expectations of the patrons and the perceptions of local review groups). All of these factors impinge on fulfillment for one or more of the discourses and so are factors that we as architects ought to be able to come to terms with—either through acceptance, which is the case now, or through active engagement, which is the implication of the model I propose.

A paradigm in this conception of practice is the work of the architects of Morphosis in the design of the restaurant Angeli on Melrose Avenue in Los Angeles, where the architects did have a hand in some of the other-than-form factors I've just named. Famously in LA in the 1980s, the menus of the restaurant featured a credit to the architects. That credit was, of course, a nod to the positioning effects that the architects' star quality could have upon the marketplace. But it was also an implicit recognition that place feeling (a concern, we now know, of both the Market and Community) is today a matter that involves not just form but publicity and graphics (I still have an Angeli tee-shirt: today, when carefully laundered, the souvenir of the architecture can outlive the architecture) and practices, not least the publicized practice of the restaurateurs giving their architects broader than usual say-so in the design of the total experience of the place.

But I've said that, as an ideal, all our design acts would be seeable by the discourses as fulfillment for them, but also as fulfillment for us architects. If Design's idea of fulfillment is to be able to see a design act as an instance of order fit for inclusion in historical narratives, then how can we see order—much less inclusion—in acts that design only knowledge or practices or mere sensation? If we architects use those tools, then many of our design acts will not be about *form* at all.

How can our works be comparable to past works if not through *form?*

To get at an answer, let me turn the question on its head: Do we really, today, think *form* a sufficient basis for ajudging comparability? I think that today, when we look back at canonical buildings, we find ourselves asking questions like, "How did people live there?" and "What role did the life of that building play in the larger culture?" and "How did the people of that time *see* that building?" These are questions that go beyond the form, the appearance of past buildings. These are questions about the very agents of place feeling and market positioning that we have seen earlier, questions about practices, knowledge, and perception.

I think it's fair to say that we are coming to feel, about the "reality" of past works, that the visible form of canonical works is an *insufficient capture of their reality.*

The insights of critical theory, as they percolate through the culture, are one factor in our coming to think this way. Critical theory teaches us to be suspicious of the mere appearance of a thing, makes us want to know the forces and practices that gave it that appearance, and what that appearance meant to the people of its time.

The allied trend of "history from below" has taught us to be suspicious of canonical monuments in general. We no longer think that stories of kings and wars capture the historical reality of a period. We now want to know how ordinary people lived then, how they thought, what they ate, wore, and believed.

The grounds for claiming the next point are shakier, but I would add our experience of *movies* to this mix of factors that condition our perception of the comparability of past works to present works. More than one cultural commentator has remarked how all the eras since the 1930s feel equally familiar to us and accessible to our understanding, while the times before that seem to have a whiff of that Foucault *strangeness* about them. The strangeness is of course because those earlier eras don't *talk* to us, in movies, the way every era since does. We feel that we know the reality of every era since the advent of the talkies. And so, holding sound movies as something of a paradigm for "reality fully captured," we find ourselves holding out for a similar kind of knowledge about eras further back.

We are coming to define "the past" in a way that renders form or appearance insufficient to capture it, and thus insufficient as a standard of comparison. To illustrate what we do expect of the past, we can turn again to the Eames Case Study house. For an architect, the "reality" of the house—those aspects of it that make it canonical—consists of much more than just its form. Its place in history also comes about because of its provenance in the Case Study program, the ideals it embodies, and the ways in which those ideals reflected both the postwar moment in America and the larger phenomenon of modernism. The tenor of the life Charles and Ray lived there is also central to our sense of the house. And our sense of the house is shaped by our knowledge of the Eameses' movies, exhibitions, and books: to see their short film *Toccata for Toy Trains* is to understand the Eameses' sensibility in a way that conditions utterly your perception of the house.

All that is the "reality" of the Case Study house to an architect, and to a critic or historian. Any of those aspects could serve, and have served, as a basis for comparing the Eames house with other works, for seating it in narratives.

We architects, I want to suggest, already do see comparability as a combination of the form of a place and the experience of it. I merely push the envelope when I propose that comparability might consist mostly, or even wholly, of *comparability of experience.*

But experience is so fleeting. What about *permanence?*

The question implies the commonsense idea that there is a real distinction between things like knowledge, practices, and sensation, and things like buildings—the difference being that buildings endure and are real while those other things are evanescent and have no real existence.

In response, let me point out that permanence in architecture is not what it used to be. One of the bases of that permanence was *institutions*. For several centuries, it was assumed that the most enduring architecture would be that which housed institutions. For the last couple of centuries, architects have believed that a rock-solid basis for designing such a building would be to make its plan a diagram of the institution's internal workings. That is the design strategy behind works as diverse in time and intention as the University of Virginia and the Salk Center. Now, though, the organization of an institution is thought of as something to be kept fluid, continually reconfigured to changes in the outer world and to the developing precepts of the science of management.

Nor do institutions today seem permanent even as entities. In the United States for the last century, the big institutions of our lives were the great corporations—IBM, US Steel, AT&T—that seemed as enduring as the government, and whose headquarters became, in recent years, a building type much talked about in architectural circles. I need not tell you the fate of such corporations in the past decade, the mergers, takeovers, downsizing, bankruptcy. My personal index of the impermanence of institutions—their unreliability as a basis for architecture—came to me each month in recent years in the form of my credit card statement from "Gulf Oil, a division of Cumberland Farms." A major institution a part of a convenience-store chain.

If corporate headquarters vanished as an important building type when corporations became "virtual," other whole classes of building vanished for the reason of advancing technology. In Boston near my apartment stands an 1890s armory, built to defend the city against (one supposes) mobs of disaffected Irish or Italians. An architectural masterpiece, it is also a true fortress, with a dry moat, thick granite walls with loop-holes for sharpshooters, and retractable iron-plate shutters for every window. It stands now ludicrous in its defensive posture against throngs of people, for the control of civil unrest now comes through means that have no permanent form: wiretaps and surveillance, mobile police patrols, helicopter overflights. A whole field of architectural effort, and commentary, was stopped in its tracks by machinery and communications.

Or take the grand banking lobby, another significant architectural commission during the past century. The crowning moment of such spaces was the huge, brushed-stainless vault door, swung open into plain view, its security mechanisms exposed behind bulletproof glass—all this to say to you the customer that the place where your money is stored is impregnably secure. Only now, of course, your money exists as electromagnetic pulses, the physicality and permanence of the vault rendered irrelevant by electronics, a deeply meaningful symbolism rendered silly by subsequent developments.

But the real challenge to the idea of permanence as coextensive with architecture comes from another quarter. Because of the way we build today, many of the forms we build are not really permanent in the usual sense of that word. Once the fabric of a building largely defended itself against deterioration. Now, increasingly, the fabric is something that must be defended, by the continual application of powered equipment. Many a modern building must be continually heated lest the foundation heave and the water pipes burst. From the ordinary sump pumps in residential basements to the sophisticated tuned dampers at the top of high-rises, buildings these days are kept permanent only because power is constantly applied to them.

What is more, the building may not be permanently habitable by us, in any meaningful sense, without the continuing application of power (HVAC, lights, communications, etc.) and ongoing renewal (light bulbs, paper towels, and so forth).

What this suggests is that there is no longer a useful distinction between an enduring fabric of a building—its "architecture"—and the equipment and people who come and go within it. The fabric has no true permanent, independent existence that can stand on its own apart from its powered equipment and the actions of its maintainers. Turn off the power and leave the building on its own and it will immediately be uninhabitable, and a little while after that, deteriorated.

This condition has real implications for our conception of architecture. We always knew, if we thought about it, that knowledge and practices required continual human "consent" for them to continue to operate in our lives. We know as well that for equipment to keep producing sensation, somebody must continually agree to input power to keep it operating. Now we see that the building itself requires a similar "consent" for its continued existence: somebody or some group must be willing continually to input effort and power into the maintenance of the building.

Put another way, all of the tools for achieving fulfillment—equipment for sensation, knowledge and practices, and buildings—are now similar in that all require continual human "consent." For any of them to continue, some group must see it as *in its interest* to expend energy or resources to keep it going.

That is why the next point is so crucial. Sanctioned impermanence is not only the condition under which we architects must design toward our conception of fulfillment. All other things being equal, a strategy of gaining fulfillment through impermanent means is in the interest of both of the discourses we transact with.

It's easy to see why the Market would prefer to use impermanent means to make its bid for substitution. If the bid failed—or if the offering found initial success but later met rejection—impermanent means would allow for a quick response: redesign the publicity, change the waiters' uniforms and presentation, modify the menu, remix the sound, redirect the lighting. Or if all else failed, with impermanent means, the marketers would not be stuck holding onto a permanent losing proposition. To cut their losses, they would merely have to stop expending resources: cancel the ongoing publicity, lay off the staff, unplug the machinery.

The Community discourse would likewise find it in its interest to hedge its bets when making a bid to the larger world for embodiment. To have a setting become beloved by its community is a task at least as iffy as marketing a new building. And even if the community does feel that the setting embodies its consensus, that consensus can shift over time. And if it were to shift, then the old embodier, if permanent, would not just be a nagging burden on resources: it would likely bear the onus, as we saw earlier, of embodying a vision of living at best discredited and at worst offensive.

None of this is to say that architecture should abandon permanence altogether. There are desires for permanence that transcend the "consensus" and "substitution" orientations of the Market and Community. And there are times—in memorials, for instance—

when we do indeed want to thrust a proposition into the future that will stand unchanged in the face of change. In this kind of architecture we see the building as a critical emissary from the present into the future, standing there speaking its message from us regardless of what the future comes to think.

This proposition does, though, challenge the idea of such an intention serving as the paradigm that defines what architecture is and does. What this analysis implies is that because of the way we build, and because of the ways of the world we build in, for a building to continue to exist in any meaningful way, it must be able continually to elicit *consent* from its constituency.

But if Design so accommodates itself to the interests of its constituencies, then what about *critique*?

The question to ask here is not *whether* Design critiques the world but *where*. I would say that the proper place for an architect to mount a critique is not through his design but through his participation in the formulation of the charge from each of the discourses.

Remember that a discourse (as we're using the term) is not a cast of characters but a frame of mind. An architect, like any person affected by the proposed building, can think in Market and Community ways and so participate in those discourses.

Remember too that it is in neither Community's interest nor the Market's interest to freeze the architect out from their discussions. For the architect to be able to respond effectively to a charge from one of the discourses, he must be able to interpret its parts in light of the whole, and vice versa. The surest way for the architect to be able to gain such an understanding is for him to be present during the synthesis of the charge. If Community and the Market want the architect to understand his charge as they do, then they ought to want him to be there as that understanding takes shape.

It is in that venue that the architect can offer his perspective on the building situation at hand. Once the charge has been formulated, though, the architect is obligated to respond to it faithfully. To use the design process post facto to critique the charge, after having had a fair hearing for his insights, would be ethically reprehensible.

None of this is to say that "critical" design can't be conducted, only that, as was the case with permanence, critique can't tenably serve as a model for practice. Schools, for example, always will and always should use design to propose conceptions critical of, or alternative to, those the larger world gives us. But when schools make those proposals, we must bear in mind that such proposals are imaginable only because the operation of one or more of the transacting discourses has been suspended. It is because of that absence of transaction that school work can demonstrate to us what can happen when Design is allowed to operate upon its own values, unconstrained by other values. Such demonstrations are useful to practitioners in their transactions with other value systems because they show so starkly what it is that *architects* believe.

The problem occurs when we architects take such demonstrations as evidence of the *superiority* of Design values over those of the Market or Community. If one comes to believe that, then one must naturally feel that those other values should not be transacted with on an equal basis but resisted from a position of superiority.

It is of course possible to hold to the position that Design should critically resist the values of the existent world. Like schools, "resistant" practices are a vital part of that ongoing conversation about what the developing practice will deem excellent. But also like schools, resistant practices operate only in special circumstances. Having no power actually to countermand the values of Community or the Market, a resistant practice can operate only where those values are willingly held in suspension. Far from being "practice against the world," a resistant, critical practice is more nearly "practice at the sufferance of the world."

And yet despite every architect's certain knowledge that critique is truly "practice as it is sometimes allowed to be," there persists among us the romantic notion of resistance being "practice as it should be." We saw some of the consequences of holding to that notion in the architects' laments of the first chapter. What was only implicit in those laments is the frustration and self-blame that afflicts architects who judge their work and themselves by this untenable, impossible standard. An architect pays a price for resistance, and it is exacted not just upon his livelihood and not just upon his happiness but upon his family and friends, his professional relationships, perhaps even his health.

That's what I could not see but could surely feel as I walked around the AIA convention. It is to free us architects from that self-reproach, as much as anything, that I've devised this theory for practice.

The good life for an architect

Against that image of the architect living a life of resistance and paying a price for it, let me propose two counter images, and with them give you a whiff of the flavor of practice under this theory.

The first image is the work of the artist Christo. When Christo does one of his environmental installations, his "art" is not just the piece itself but every transaction required to realize it. Esthetically subversive as they might be, Christo's works are consented to by every possible affected group or authority. He secures these clearances with publicity, endless meetings, visualizations and all of his great personal charm. He even raises the money to realize the work and, vitally important, insure it against liability. Then there is the massive work of coordinating the construction: recruiting the volunteers, training them, feeding and housing them, and keeping all the workers in communication with each other. And there is the documentation, recording the entire event—its preparation, its construction, and the experience of the work in place—for in a manner of days, Christo will oversee the dismantling of the piece, removing all trace of it from the site.

The example of Christo invites us architects to see the transactions we do in practice not as a means to art but as our art itself. A practice conducted like his would see the building project as not burdened by but *consisting of* the client meetings, the public hearings, the publicity, ceremonies, music, lights, tee-shirts—everything, in short, that is required in order for the *anticipated experience to occur.* All of that, under this conception of practice, would be "the architecture."

As a second alternative to the notion of a resistant practice, I would like to counterpose the image of Charles and Ray Eames and the ways they conducted their practice. In the terms of this theory, we could talk about their Case Study house as *fulfilling* all three of our discourses. Seen as an instance of order, the house has certainly figured in plenty of Design narratives. Without question the house is an embodiment of the Eameses' values about living, even the embodiment of a "consensus" of ongoing conversations between them and their associates and friends as a community. And the whole genesis of the house, and of the Case Study program itself, was as a proposition to the marketplace to substitute this kind of house for the typical wood-framed California ranch house (a proposal that was not by any means wholly rejected, its partial acceptance being in fact the subject of quite a few narratives, Design and otherwise).

We could also talk about how fulfillment, in all three discourses, was sought through those nonpermanent means other than form: how the Eames gave the Design discourse canonical photographs and articles, eminently ready for critical narratives; how the Eameses' work in furniture and exhibition design became part of the stories Design could imagine about the house. And how knowledge of all that helped position the house with a certain segment of the marketplace.

But most telling for us are the ways apart from form that the Eameses used to achieve embodiment of their vision of living, Community's concept of fulfillment. We have already heard the tale of my afternoon with Ray—the tea, the roses, the pastries, the sunset from the terrace. The Eameses designed all those things and more— Christmas cards, photographs, home movies, interviews, parties—to condition the experience of the house for themselves and for the Community consisting of their friends and admirers.

The reason this observation is the most telling for us is this: What the Eameses did to achieve fulfillment, in all three of our discourses, is no different from *what we architects habitually do for themselves*. When we architects design our environments (and photograph them, and write or talk about them), we almost always have one eye aimed toward their inclusion in some imagined critical essay. We see our homes and offices as marketing tools, and we calculate what we do to them, at least in part, on the basis of what results we might get for what outlay of resources.

But most revealing of our true motivations are the efforts we expend at the embodiment of the values of our little community of family or companions (or imagined companions). Like the Eameses we shape the forms, but we also direct the lighting, mix the music, choose the menu, arrange the flowers and objects. We design the ceremonies that will occur in this setting of ours: we choose the napery, the china, the cutlery, determine the timing of the courses, try to influence the dress and practices of the guests and even of ourselves the hosts. And over all this we cast an aura of publicity, through our design of Christmas cards, party invitations, carefully choreographed articles in the local newspaper.

All of this we do for ourselves, in the interest of achieving fulfillment for the three orientations to the environment that we architects inhabit as real people. And yet, when called upon to perform the same triple service for our clients, we architects constrain ourselves to the provision of *form,* the permanent stuff of "architecture" as it was exemplified to us in those Parthenon-to-Palladio courses we all took in school.

A purpose of this theory has been to argue against this conception, not just this conception of architecture but this conception of what it is we architects do. I've been constructing a theory under which architects could do for others, in practice, what they so naturally do in life for themselves. Life and practice conducted to the same set of principles. The very definition of the good life for an architect.

And one last thing. It is inevitable in the life of an architect that she will see her works abandoned or changed out of all recognition. Under this conception of architecture that I'm promoting, the goal of the architect is not the realization of the form but the achievement of fulfillment—for herself as a speaker for Design and for her transacting others as speakers for Community and the Market. If an architect sees architecture in these terms, she will realize that fulfillment for her own discourse will be based on the achieved state of her design, frozen for all future potential narrative in its initial, architect-designed form. But from the same conception she will see that fulfillment for the other discourses will not be based in the recorded initial state of the design, but will be have to come out of the ongoing lived experience of the setting she designs. For people thinking in those other discourses, when the setting she designed no longer achieves fulfillment for their perspectives, the building will have ceased to participate in their lives. For them the setting she designed will have ceased to live.

At that point, our imagined architect would say to herself about her creation—its form, its publicity, the ceremonies enacted there, the knowledge, memories, and records of its existence—she would say with regret but equanimity: Let it go.

All of it was and will be architecture.

This is how things must be and probably should be.

It's going to be all right.

Notes

Chapter 1b

1. Alasdair MacIntyre, *After Virtue* (Notre Dame: University of Notre Dame Press, 1981), 104.

2. Ibid., 74.

Chapter 2a

1. Michel Foucault, *The Order of Things* (New York: Vintage Books, 1973), xv.

2. MacIntyre, 52.

3. Leon Battista Alberti, *On the Art of Building in Ten Books*, trans. Joseph Rykwert, Neil Leach, and Robert Tavernor (Cambridge: MIT Press, 1988), 5.

4. Alberti, 125. Note that Alberti makes no judgment about whether you choose to model your life on that of the tyrant or the private citizen, and that is to be expected. You could make such a judgment only if you believed in the existence of a universal standard of conduct that applied to everyone. Alberti does not believe that. The fact that Florentines might have declared the "private citizen" model to be proper in Florence says nothing about what should be proper in Mantua.

5. MacIntyre, 59.

6. Alberti, 126.

7. Ibid., 156.

8. Alberti himself says, "I am of the opinion that there is nothing, aside from virtue, to which a man should devote more care, more effort and attention, than to the acquisition of a good home to shelter himself and his family" (Alberti, 18).

9. Information on the operations of the Chaux saltworks comes from two sources: Anthony Vidler, *Claude-Nicolas Ledoux* (Cambridge: MIT Press, 1990); and Mark K. Deming, *La saline royale d'Arc et Senans* (Arc-et-Senans: Fondation Claude Nicolas Ledoux, 1986).

10. Clearly, however, Chaux did function as a salt factory (though perhaps not as productively as its backers had hoped), and did so right up to the beginning of this century (Vidler, 132).

11. Reyner Banham, *The Architecture of the Well-Tempered Environment* (London: Architectural Press, 1969), 75–83.

12. Ibid., 84.

13. G. F. Bodley, "Architectural Study and the Examination Test," in *Architecture: A Profession or an Art?*, ed. R. Norman Shaw and T. G. Jackson (London: John Murray, 1892), 64.

14. T. G. Jackson, "Introduction," in *Architecture: A Profession?*, x.

15. Ernest Newton, "Architects and Surveyors," in *Architecture: A Profession?*, 90.

16. Ibid., 88–92.

17. Jackson, xiv.

18. Ibid., xii.

19. David C. Lewis, *The Public Image of Henry Ford* (Detroit: Wayne State University Press, 1976), 213.

20. Ibid., 129.

21. Robert Lacey, *Ford: The Men and the Machine* (Boston: Little, Brown and Co., 1986), 285.

22. Lewis, 177.

23. Ibid., 115.

24. Ibid., 215.

25. Lacey, 210.

26. Henry Ford, *My Life and Work* (New York: Doubleday, Page & Co., 1922), 73.

27. Ibid., 149.

28. The nearest analogue for the fanaticism people felt about their Model T's might be the enthusiasm many felt about their first personal computer. As was the case with the Model T, the manufacturer kept offering "upgrades" for your old machine. As with the Model T, companies other than the manufacturer offered whole lines of

accessories you could add on to your machine, for looks or performance or just to personalize it. And numerous clubs formed (today called "user groups"), ostensibly to share information but really just to act out members' enthusiasm at being involved in something all felt to be important.

29. Ford, 77.

30. Ibid., 72.

31. Lacey, 290.

32. Ford, 124, 129.

33. Lacey, 288.

34. Lewis, 203.

Chapter 2b

1. Alberti, 146.

2. Ibid., 149.

3. MacIntyre, 172.

4. Ibid.

5. Ibid.

6. Alberti, 149–150.

7. Some of these thoughts are surprisingly prescient. He advocates the use of iron in construction in order to save the oak forests for "indispensable uses" (shipbuilding being deemed, in his time, one such critical use) (333). He says that at some future time the public will rebel against lavish expenditures for public buildings (though for him the rebellion will result in the demand for "four plain walls in rubble and stucco which will give repose to the eye and not empty the purse") (100). And he echoes, in more eloquent terms than mine, a point I made earlier, that by not adhering to "reason" in design, the architect renders his work subject to capricious whims: "Anyone may demand this or that alteration according to the whims of the moment." When this happens, architecture "falls into the category of *objets de luxe*—the nicknacks that one buys or gets rid of according to the fashion of the day" (128).

8. Eugène Emmanuel Viollet-le-Duc, *Discourses on Architecture* (New York: Grove Press, 1959), reprint, 265.

9. Ibid.

10. Ibid.

11. Ibid., 266.

12. Mark Girouard, *Life in the English Country House* (New Haven: Yale University Press, 1978), 2ff.

13. Ibid., 46.

14. Ibid., 88.

15. Ibid., 99.

16. Ibid., 138.

17. Ibid., 146.

18. Ibid., 184.

19. Ibid., 185.

20. Ibid., 204.

21. Too many cues from the architecture would in fact have undercut their enjoyment. One aspect of elegance is the ability to do the expected without being cued. Another aspect is apparent effortlessness, but if too much direction is given, the act truly *is* effortless. Effortlessness "tells" only when it is known that some difficulty is involved, that a faux pas is possible.

22. A present-day near analogue to this kind of categorical thinking might be seen in the layout of the electrical panel board for a large house. In no way does the arrangement of the board correspond to the plan of the house, much less to how the house is used. The determining category is "capacity and type of circuit breaker or fuse," the governing considerations being ease of installation and correctness of replacement. And so the big fuse or breaker for the kitchen range is right next to the one for the heat pump, even though the stove and heater are nowhere near each other, nor are they used in close conjunction with each other.

23. Girouard also notes this growing unease about servants. "Their presence . . . had been taken for granted in earlier decades, but now grated on people's growing sense of privacy" (219).

24. Girouard, 231–232.

25. Ibid., 219.

26. Ibid., 218–219.

27. Quoted in ibid., 285.

28. Gary Wills, in his *Lincoln at Gettysburg*, shows how before the Civil War, the Constitution was viewed as the proper framework for American values—the Constitution that contained within it tacit approval of slavery. But Lincoln, in his Gettysburg Address, substituted the notion that the Declaration of Independence was the true founding proposition of the nation, implying that the Constitution was only an imperfect (and thus mutable) instrument for implementing that proposition, and that the true work of the nation was to move toward the achievement of the proposition, "that all men are created equal."

29. Charles Howard Shinn, *Mining Camps: A Study in American Frontier Government* (New York: Charles Scribner's Sons, 1884; reprint, Gloucester, MA: Peter Smith, 1970), 110.

30. Josiah Royce, *California: A Study of American Character* (Boston: Houghton Mifflin Co., 1886), 279–280. Royce does go on to add a cautionary note, but one that does not undercut his thesis about the American character: "But we must still insist: all this view of the mining life is one-sided, because this good order, widely spread as it often undoubtedly was, was still in its nature unstable, since it had not been won as a prize of social devotion, but only attained by a sudden feat of instinctive cleverness. The social order is, however, something that instinct must make in its essential elements, by a sort of first intention, but that only voluntary devotion can secure against corruption" (281).

Royce here echoes, in his own way, MacIntyre's distinction between practices and the institutions by which those practices interact with the larger world.

31. Royce, 290. The rule seemed fair, we can speculate, because it gave due weight to the two prime motivations of the mining camp: discovery (which had brought the men individually to the camp) and equity (without which there could not be the teamwork that made discovery more profitable). The half-ounce nugget, by the way, would have been worth six dollars in cash or eight dollars in trade to a man who might expect his one-quarter share of a day's take to be around twenty-five dollars (Shinn, 115–116).

32. Rhys Isaac, *The Transformation of Virginia, 1740–1790* (Chapel Hill: University of North Carolina Press, 1982).

33. Royce, 280 (italics mine).

34. Alexis de Tocqueville, *Democracy in America*, ed. Richard D. Heffner (New York: New American Library, 1956), 99–100.

35. Ibid., 98.

Chapter 3

1. MacIntyre, 187.

2. Ibid., 188.

3. Ibid., 190–191.

4. Ibid., 188–189. The fact that people can come close to imagining what it's like to run a marathon and therefore almost know the experience for what it is—this only demonstrates the correctness of MacIntyre's restrictive definition of a practice. Running a marathon is not a very complex "practice," and so when one empathizes from one's own experiences of endurance, one is probably not too far off the mark of a true appreciation of what the runner has done. With more complex endeavors, those that would pass MacIntyre's test, analogies from one's own out-of-the-practice experiences fall farther afield from what true practitioners think and feel.

5. Ibid., 190.

6. Ibid., 194.

7. Ibid., 193–194.

8. Ibid., 222.

9. Ibid.

10. MacIntyre reminds us that we live out our lives in the light of conceptions about the future, "a future in which certain possibilities beckon us forward and others repel us, some seem already foreclosed, and others perhaps inevitable" (215).

> ... like characters in a fictional narrative, we do not know what will happen next, but nonetheless our lives have a certain form which projects itself towards our future.
> If the narrative of our individual and social lives is to continue intelligibly—and either type of narrative may lapse into unintelligibility—it is always both the case that there are constraints on how the story can continue and that within those constraints there are indefinitely many ways that it can continue. (216)

Chapter 4

1. Daniel Kemmis, *Community and the Politics of Place* (Norman, OK: University of Oklahoma Press, 1990), 66.

2. Roger Fisher and William Ury, *Getting to Yes: Negotiating Agreement Without Giving In* (New York: Penguin Books, 1983).

3. Kemmis, 66.

4. Ibid.

5. Ibid., 81.

Chapter 5

1. I need here to express my gratitude to Frederick Turner for his book *Spirit of Place: The Making of an American Literary Landscape* (San Francisco: Sierra Club Books, 1989). The book not only introduced me to the Nebraska Panhandle and the author Mari Sandoz, but convinced me that this enterprise of place analysis made sense and gave me an image of how such an analysis might sound.

2. I owe knowledge of this fact to Tom Chastain, friend, colleague, and native Nebraskan.

3. You will also find, alongside the roads, at least a dozen Sandoz mailboxes and Sandoz farm signs—evidence of the continuing presence of the descendants of both Old Jules and his wife, and the many immigrants they helped settle. And from this you might suspect "Old Jules Country" to be something of a cottage industry of the Sandoz family, which to a certain extent it is. But in that region you can also drop into your conversation with any local person a reference to Old Jules or Mari Sandoz,

and you'll get instant recognition, precise guidance to an obscure site, or a book-engendered recollection. (No great outpouring of welcome or bubbling enthusiasm, mind you. This is the Plains after all.) Even if a little propped-up, the presence of Old Jules is nonetheless felt in this region, is a part of its sense of place.

4. A part of Jules's resentment came out of the memorialized Well Accident. As a result of a practical joke gone tragically wrong, Jules was tumbled to the bottom of a well he and his brother were digging, crushing his foot in the fall. Taken with fright, the brother fled the scene, leaving Jules for dead. He lay there for a number of days until rescued by a passing party of soldiers, who carried him to Fort Robinson, forty miles away. There he was treated by the camp physician (who was, of all people, Dr. Walter Reed). But the damage to the foot had been too long unattended; it would never fully heal. Jules would never again walk unaided, and for the rest of his life his foot would be encased in a grotesque boot, oversized to contain the swelling—a devastating blow to a young man who had taken pride in both his appearance and his agility. When, after months, he returned to his farm, he seemed to his neighbors to have aged into a bitter decrepitude. He was ever after called *Old* Jules.

5. My account of homesteading and the Rectangular Survey come from Roy M. Robbins, *Our Landed Heritage: The Public Domain, 1776–1970* (Lincoln: University of Nebraska Press, 1976).

6. Mari Sandoz, *Old Jules* (New York: Hastings House, 1935; reprint, Lincoln: University of Nebraska Press, 1985), 21n.

7. In regions where settlement had already begun, you might run the process backward: go to the land office, note which quarter-sections were still unclaimed, do a quick reconnoiter of them, and then come back and stake a claim to your choice. If you chose to settle in advance of the surveys, you maximized your choice of sites, but you ran a risk: once the surveyors ran their lines, you might find your house in one quarter-section and the bulk of your fields—or that spring—in another.

8. Sandoz, 21n.

9. Ibid., 25.

10. Ibid., 26.

11. Jane Smiley, *A Thousand Acres* (New York: Fawcett Columbine, 1991), 3–4. That an accurate map can be drawn from just Jane Smiley's words is a feature of the Rectangular System. We can be rather certain, for example, that the Ericsons' land is a half-section, a full section cut in two by a north-south line, the imagined thousand-acre farm being a mile north-south by a mile-and-a-half east-west.

Seeing land in these geometric terms—and living in a landscape laid out in such a way—can condition even how we see our bodies in spaces closer to hand. A former student of mine recalled how her mother, in her farmhouse in Iowa, would answer queries about the location of some utensil in her kitchen with phrases like, "It's two drawers north of the sink." And in York, Nebraska, the owners of Heide Auto Shine think it totally sufficient to hang a large sign on the side of their building that states, with no arrow, "Entrance East Door."

12. Sandoz, 30.

13. Ibid., 41.

14. Ibid., 71.

15. Ibid., 70.

16. Ibid., 98–99.

17. Ibid., 102.

18. Ibid., 144.

19. Ibid., 163.

20. Ibid., 234–235.

21. Ibid., 192.

22. Ibid., 267.

23. Helen Winter Stauffer, *Mari Sandoz, Story Catcher of the Plains* (Lincoln: University of Nebraska Press, 1982), 56.

24. Ibid., 29.

25. Sandoz, 216.

26. Ibid., 259.

27. Ibid., 241. So as not to leave you with the impression of Old Jules as a complete sadist, let me complete the quote:

> The mother dragged her from her nook. "Ach, can't you ever do anything right?"
> But Old Jules, standing around with his hands in his pockets, his pipe drawing well, was expansive. "Let her go," he said, and lifted the girl upon a chair so she might look into a round silver ball that made her face bulge like Mrs. Fluckiger's. (241)

28. Ibid., 251.

29. Ibid., 402.

30. Ibid., 338.

31. Ibid., 354.

Index

Aalto, Alvar, Seinajoki library, 144
Alberti, Leon Battista, 39–44, 61–63
American Institute of Architects, 1, 25,
  101
Architects
  attitude toward design of, 2, 9, 13
  dress of, 1–3
  education of, 6–9
  "good life" for, 164–167
Architecture: A Profession or an Art?, 51–54
Automatic teller machines, 80–83,
  151–153

Back Bay Station (Boston), 34
Banham, Reyner, 48–51, 56
Bentham, Jeremy, 47–48
Borges, Jorge Luis, 40
Boston Marathon, as a practice, 89–90

Chaux, Royal Saltworks of, 44–47, 71, 73
Chess, as a practice, 89
Christo (artist), 164
Community discourse
  defined, 84–85
  in operation, 102–110, 116–119, 150–
  153, 161–162
Contractors, in production of buildings,
  24–25
Critical theory, in architects' education,
  8–9, 157
Critique, in architecture, 162–164

Democracy, influence on design, 64–65,
  73

Design discourse
  in operation, 87–100, 102–110, 116–
  119, 155–158, 162–167
Design reasoning, 18–19, 22–23
De Tocqueville, Alexis, 84
Discourse, 28, 60
Disneyland, 135–136

Eames, Ray and Charles, 100, 158
  life at Case Study house, 3, 87
  life as model for practice, 97, 100,
  164–166
Epistème, 40
Ethical closure, in practice, 106–107
Excellence, in practice, 91–92
Exhibition design, 136

Florence (Italy), social organization of,
  42–43, 62–63
Ford, Henry, 54–59
Foucault, Michel, 40

Gehry, Frank, 135
Getting to Yes, 111
Giedion, Siegfried, 6, 95
Girouard, Mark, 65–77
"Good life for an architect," 88,
  164–167
Goods external and internal to practice,
  88–91

Haddon Hall, 67
Hadrian's Villa, 135
Hagley Hall, 72

Here-there sense
  as basis for communication, 122–123
  as basis for consensus, 119
  defined, 118
  engendered by:
    attention to apparatus, 152, 155
    cartographic knowledge, 150
    conventions of behavior, 151, 154
    cultural practices, 151, 154
    direct sensation, 152, 154
    economic practices, 151
    geographic knowledge, 150
    historical moments, 150
    literature, 150
    managed sensation, 152, 154–155
    publicity, 153
    scientific knowledge, 150
    shared memory or knowledge, 150,
      153
    shared practices, 151–152, 154
    spatial sense, 152, 155
  varieties of
    bordered sense, 125–127, 141–144,
      151, 153
    continuous sense, 142–143, 149, 153
    interlocked sense, 132, 143, 149
    isolated sense, 133–134, 140, 149,
      151–153
    only-adjacent sense, 135–136, 140,
      149
    pervasive sense, 128, 132–133, 145,
      149, 152
    related sense, 138–139, 142, 146, 149
History and criticism, construction of,
  93–98
Homestead Act of 1863, 129–130
Houghton Hall, 69

Inhabitation, as basis for Community
  consensus, 115–116
Institutions, contrasted with practices,
  91–92, 106–107
Interests, contrasted with positions,
  111–113

Judgmental work, in production of
  buildings, 102–108

Katsura Imperial Palace, 132
Kemmis, Daniel, 111–116

Le Corbusier, 55, 59, 133
Ledoux, Claude-Nicolas, 43–48, 71

Liability, in architectural practice,
  106–107

MacIntyre, Alasdair, 35–36, 41–44, 88–
  93, 96–97, 174
Management, methods of, 34–36
Market discourse
  defined, 59–60
  in operation, 102–108, 110, 116–119,
    153–155, 161–162
Marshcourt (Edwin Lutyens), 75
Missoula, Montana, 111–115, 121
Model T Ford, 55–57
Modernism, in architects' education,
  6–7
Moore, Charles, 32
Mormon diggings (California), 78–80

Narrative continuity, as principle of history and practice, 95–100, 157–158
Nebraska Sand Hills, 123–127, 143–147,
  150
Niobrara River, 129, 143

Panopticon (Jeremy Bentham), 47–48
Pantheon, 134
Paradigms of order, 18, 32–33
Permanence, in architecture, 158–162
Pevsner, Nikolaus, 6, 95
Photography, in architecture, 31–32
Place, sense of, 121–122, 153. *See also*
  Here-there sense
Positions, contrasted with interests,
  111–113
Practices
  contrasted with institutions, 91–92,
    106–107
  defined, 88
Professionalism, crisis of, 10–12

Rationalization, 51–54, 55, 59
Rectangular Survey of U.S., 129–132,
  150, 153, 175
Reed, Dr. Walter, 175
Resale value, 20–22
Rotunda (University of Virginia), 134
Royal Victoria Hospital, Belfast, 48–51,
  56
Royce, Josiah, 78–80, 83–84, 173

Sandoz, Jules, 122, 127–146
Sandoz, Mari, 122–147, 176
Scarpa, Carlo, 132

Smiley, Jane, 131, 150
Sunset magazine, 32
Synthetic work, in production of build-
    ings, 102, 109–116
    of Community discourse, 110–116
    of Design discourse, 108–110
    of Market discourse, 110

Taste, 28–29
Telos, 41–44
Tempietto (Bramante), 134
Tradition
    as focus of architects' education, 7–8
    and practice, 92–93
Transactional work, 102–103, 116–119
Turner, Frederick, 174

Values
    of architects, 20–23, 25, 27, 29–31
    at automatic teller machines, 80–83
    of clients, 20–24, 27, 29
    of commerce, 20, 23, 26–28
    of contractors, 24–25, 27
    embodied in English country houses,
        66–77
    of Florentine society, 42–43, 62–63
    of gold miners, 79–80
    of maintenance workers, 34–36
    of Management, 34–36
    of the public, 37–38
Variations, in music and architecture,
    33–34
Viollet-le-Duc, Eugène Emmanuel,
    63–65
Virtù, 40–43, 62

Wills, Gary, 172
Wright, Frank Lloyd, 2–3, 97, 100, 132